PENGUIN HANDBOOKS

THE STANISLAVSKI SYSTEM

Sonia Moore was born in Russia. She attended
the universities of Kiev and Moscow, the Studio of the Kiev Solovstov Theater, and the
Third Studio of the Moscow Art Theater, and
has degrees from conservatories in Rome. She
now lives in New York City, where she teaches
at the Sonia Moore Studio of the Theater and
is Artistic Director of ACSTA 1, the repertory
company of the American Center for Stanislavski Theater Art, which she founded.

D0638928

Also by Sonia Moore

TRAINING AN ACTOR:
THE STANISLAVSKI SYSTEM IN CLASS

NEW
REVISED EDITION

The Stanislavski System

THE PROFESSIONAL
TRAINING OF AN ACTOR

DIGESTED FROM THE TEACHINGS OF

Konstantin S. Stanislavski

BY

Sonia Moore

(Originally published as *The Stanislavski Method*)

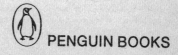

PENGUIN BOOKS

Penguin Books Ltd, Harmondsworth,
Middlesex, England
Penguin Books, 625 Madison Avenue,
New York, New York 10022, U.S.A.
Penguin Books Australia Ltd, Ringwood,
Victoria, Australia
Penguin Books Canada Limited, 2801 John Street,
Markham, Ontario, Canada L3R 1B4
Penguin Books (N.Z.) Ltd, 182–190 Wairau Road,
Auckland 10, New Zealand

First published in the United States of America
as *The Stanislavski Method*
by The Viking Press 1960
Published, with revisions, as *The Stanislavski System* 1965
The Stanislavski System, New Revised Edition,
published in a hardbound and a paperbound edition 1974
Paperbound edition reprinted 1974, 1975, 1976
Published in Penguin Books 1976
Reprinted 1977, 1978, 1979

LIBRARY OF CONGRESS CATALOGING IN PUBLICATION DATA
Moore, Sonia.
  The Stanislavski system.
  (A Penguin handbook)
  First published in 1960 under title: The Stanislavski method.
  Bibliography: p. xix.
  Includes index.
  1. Stanislavski method. I. Title.
[PN2062.M6 1976]   792'.028   76-48183
ISBN 0 14 046.259 7

Printed in the United States of America by
Offset Paperback Mfrs., Inc., Dallas, Pennsylvania
Set in Linotype Caledonia

Contents

Preface
by Sir John Gielgud

———————

I have never really believed that acting can be taught. Yet, when I remember what a clumsy beginner I was myself and how greatly I have been influenced, all through my long stage career, by the fine directors and players with whom I have been fortunate enough to be associated, I cannot deny the advantage of teaching, provided it can be followed up by hard personal experience. Let nobody imagine, however, that he can learn to act from reading books, however intelligent or profound they may be, about the art of acting.

All creative art can be studied, of course. When one is young, one imitates the players one most admires— as artists copy great pictures in the galleries. But, as the theater is an imitation of life, it is as ephemeral and intangible as life itself (in a way that music, painting, and literature are not), and it changes in every decade and generation. One cannot copy acting, or even what seems to be the method of acting. One has to experiment and discover one's own way of expression for oneself, and one never ceases to be dissatisfied. The quality and development of one's work changes with the degree of responsiveness and sureness of technique which one has acquired over the years. One is affected, too, by the style and quality of the work in hand, the respect or dissatisfaction one may have with one's material, and by one's own personal reactions to directors and fellow players, to the author, to the play itself.

There are so many lessons in the theater to be learned: application, concentration, self-discipline, the use of the voice and body, imagination, observation, simplification, self-criticism. Often the "tradition" of the theater seems to be at odds with the modern expression of original contemporary acting. I believe that one is as important as the other and that one should study and learn from both. One's basic technical equipment should be perfected in order to enable one to relax, to simplify, to cut away dead wood.

Just as one moves, in real life, from one phase to another, experiencing almost imperceptible developments along the road as one gets older and one's personal and professional experiences lead one to make new discoveries about oneself and life in general, so it is hard to pin down on paper any practical guide to help an individual actor to select the best means of discovering the wellsprings of his art—how he can draw from his own sensitivity the power to command an audience and fascinate them by his interpretation of emotions given him in a particular form by the playwright and presented by him with the guidance of the director. Since he is not the sole creator, but only an instrument working in an uncertain medium (gloriously flexible yet desperately fallible), he needs all the more to have his physical and vocal means under strict control. He must think about his work in the many hours when he is not actually practicing it, about how to cherish his powers of imagination so that he can summon them at will just at the time he needs them. He has to perform before a living audience eight times a week, after achieving a more or less finished performance in the three or four short weeks at his disposal for rehearsal, working perhaps with a director and actors with whom he may not be in sympathy. Even before this he may have had to convince a director, in a few short minutes, that he is competent to play a role for which many others are also being considered.

This book is full of good and useful observations on the study and practice of acting. It says, simply and clearly, many wise things about the art of the theater. Stanislavski's two great books are complicated and sometimes difficult—at any rate for a young actor—to digest in full. Here is an admirable précis of some of his practical wisdom; a still further proof, if one is needed, of the legacy he has left behind to carry on his own example and devotion to the theater which he served so greatly.

Foreword
by Joshua Logan

Perhaps Konstantin Stanislavski was a legend before his death in 1938. He is certainly a legend now. All over the world actors, directors, students, and teachers of acting are quoting his writings and following his teachings. Here in America new words have sprung up in theater language. For years the phrase "Stanislavski's method" was used in theatrical conversations. Now it's simply "the method." We hear phrases like "he's a method actor," "method writing," "method directing." All this, I believe, has stimulated interest in the theater and is producing some great results.

How did all of this start? Who put the word "method" into our language? Who was Stanislavski? What did he really believe? What did he really teach?

In the winter of 1930 and 1931, I had the unique opportunity of studying with Stanislavski in his studio home in Moscow and of watching him direct rehearsals. Along with my fellow student the late Charles Leatherbee I had tea with the great man and his lovely wife each day after rehearsals. I also met and talked with Nemirovich-Danchenko, the equally illustrious co-director of the Moscow Art Theater, and the Great actors of the day who were then performing in the Moscow Art Theater repertory. Among the ones we got to know were Leonidov, Moskvin, Kachalov, and Mme. Knipper-Chekhova (the widow of the great Anton Chekhov).

On several afternoons a week we would sit for three or four hours at Stanislavski's side in his studio home while he conducted rehearsals for the Stanislavski Opera, a project which was occupying most of his time during that winter. At night we attended performances of the Moscow Art Theater, and when we had exhausted that repertory we began visiting the other theaters of the rich Russian theatrical season. We saw the performances and met the artists of the Vakhtangov and Maly Theaters and especially of the startling Vsevolod Meyerhold Theater. Some of these men had been students of Stanislavski previously but were now working out their own systems and directing their own companies.

On our first night in Moscow we saw a play directed by Stanislavski himself, and it was an extraordinary surprise to us. The play was *The Marriage of Figaro* by Beaumarchais, and it was done with a racy, intense, farcical spirit which we had not associated with Stanislavski. It was as broad comedy playing and directing as anything we had ever seen. The high-style members of the cast in flashing colored costumes

would run, pose, prance, caress, faint, stutter in
confusion, and play out all the intricate patterns of the
French farce with a kind of controlled frenzy.

We were stunned. Was this the Stanislavski of the
famous method? Was this the work of the great
teacher of "affective memory"? It was our first shock
at the realization that Stanislavski was a human
being—not a distant god—that he was first and
foremost the interpreter of the author's play. Up to
that minute we had thought of him as a remote
philosopher who had envisioned a mystic method of
acting. Now we realized he was also a practical man.

In the weeks and months that followed, we saw
many plays directed by Stanislavski, including *The
Cherry Orchard* with Mme. Chekhova in the leading
role and the part originated by Stanislavski now being
played by Kachalov. This, of course, was true Stanislavski—moody, thoughtful, and emotional. But it had
an underlying earthy humor which was another surprise to us. There were often lusty physical jokes. I can
remember Moskvin as Epikhodov watching the de-
parting family talking while he nailed together some
crates, his attention so fixed on the touching scene that
he was constantly hitting his finger instead of the nail.
All through Stanislavski's work there was a strong
sense of humor, and it was boldly stated.

On the other hand, *Czar Fyodor Ióannovich* was a
pageant. Moskvin played the leading role in a serio-
comic way that reminded me often of Chaplin. This
pitiful story of the feeble-minded and ineffectual czar
even though robed and bejeweled to a dazzling

magnificence, was human and tragic, yet always pathetically comic.

Three Fat Men, a Stanislavski-supervised Soviet piece, was somewhat in the style of our modern cartoon motion pictures. The three fat men were three actors blown up with papier-mâché and stuffing to resemble three gross caricatures. They represented the Church, Capitalism, and the Army, and it was all done with the exaggerated style of a children's fairy tale.

Such political plays were forced on Stanislavski at the time by a Soviet director who had been assigned to the Moscow Art Theater, and, in order to function, Stanislavski had to include one Soviet play every so often in the Moscow Art repertoire. Yet each production was produced with the same care and vitality that he gave to the classics.

An outstanding memory to me is the production of Leo Tolstoi's *Resurrection* directed by Nemirovich-Danchenko. Kachalov played the author of the play and walked through the elaborate production speaking the emotions of the actors when they were not speaking themselves. The director took full advantage of the revolving stage at the Moscow Art Theater, and a great deal of the effect of this play was visual. We were impressed by the theatricality of the Moscow Art Theater. We had expected it to be predominantly an actors' theater; instead we found a theater that was shared by the director, the designer, the musician, and above all the author.

In watching Stanislavski rehearse, I saw him making experiments in improvisation. He was directing an opera with young students, and he was trying to break down the cliché gestures and grimaces that had been taught them by singing, dancing, and diction teachers. It was a battle of egos, constant complaining by the actors that they could not sing if they were forced to take this or that position, insistent encouragement from Stanislavski—"Go on! You can do it! Make the tone! Sing!" When the effect had been reached, he was quick to praise.

We asked Stanislavski about the method. "Create your own method," he said to us. "Don't depend slavishly on mine. Make up something that will work for you! But keep breaking traditions, I beg you."

As you can see from reading Mrs. Moore's book, Stanislavski was a complete man of the theater. His teachings encompass voice, diction, dancing, voice tone, singing, make-up, costume, wigs—all the various physical things that would change an actor's shape, form, and size to make him suit his character better.

Mrs. Moore has made a digest in her own words of many of the things Stanislavski talked about and wrote about. It will help actors and students of drama to understand something of Stanislavski's teachings.

Most of all, as Mrs. Moore points out, Stanislavski did not want the method to be an end in itself, but simply a means to an end. It suggests a way of finding personal truth in the creation of a character.

But to enjoy one's creativity to excess, to fall in love with one's inspiration, was furthest from Stanislavski's belief. When I left him that summer he wrote on the photograph he gave me, "Love the art in yourself, not yourself in the art."

Author's Note
on the New Revised Edition

The revisions in this volume are based on my further research in works by Russian theater experts on the Stanislavski System and on my own experience in applying their developments to training actors in America. The changes place more emphasis on the actor's command of his body, to make it capable of immediate expression of the inner processes; on rejecting isolated study of the elements of the System; on analysis of events on stage; on establishing the emotional memory (or affective memory) as the only source for authentic experience on stage, while rejecting the forcing of actors' emotions; and on establishing the method of physical actions as the *key* to the emotional memory and to organic behavior on stage.

My observations are derived from many works published in Moscow, including:

My Life in Art, by K. S. Stanislavski (1925, 1928).

Actors Discuss Vakhtangov, compiled by H. Kherson-ski (1940). *Glikeria Fedotova*, by Georg Goyan (1940). *Complete Works of Stanislavski*, eight volumes (1945–1961). *Ivan Moskvin on the Stage of the Moscow Art Theater*, by .V. Y. Vilenkin (1946). *Stanislavski at Rehearsal*, by V. Toporkov (1950). *Maria Nokolaevna Ermolova*, by S. N. Durylin (1953). *Vassily Ivanovitch Kachalov*, compiled and edited by V. Y. Vilenkin (1954). *The Moscow Art Theater*, edited by N. Chuskin (1955). *Stanislavski's Theatrical Legacy*, edited by E. Grabar, S. Durylin, and P. Markov (1955). *The Directorial Lessons of Vakhtangov*, by N. M. Gorchakov (1957). *The Directorial Lessons of K. S. Stanislavski*, by N. M. Gorchakov (1958). *K. S. Stanislavski on the Director's Work with an Actor*, by N. M. Gorchakov (1958). *Museum of the Moscow Art Theater* (1958). *Eugene Vakhtangov: Materials and Articles* (1959). *Technology of an Actor's Art*, by P. Erchov (1959). *Theater Ethics of Stanislavski*, by Y. Kalashnikov (1960). *In the Contemporary Theater*, by A. Anastasiev (1961). *The Mastership of an Actor*, by M. A. Venetzia-nova (1961). *The Director's Art Today*, by Y. Zavadski, A. Popov, K. Knebel, B. Pokrovski, A. Lobanov, N. Slonova, G. Georgievski, K. Ird, O. Efremov, V. Kommissarjevski (1962). *The Method of K. S. Stanislavski and the Physiology of Emotions*, by P. V. Simonov (1962). *Discussions about Stanislavski*, by Vladimir Prokofiev (1963). *Innovations in Soviet Theater*, by A. Anastasiev, G. Boyardjeff, L. Obraztzova, K. Rudnitzki (1963). *Recollections and Reflections about Theater*, by Alexei Popov (1963). *The System of Stanislavski and the Problems of Dramaturgy*, by Vl.

Blok (1963). *Vakhtangov*, by K. H. Khersonski (1963). *Mastership of an Actor and Director*, by B. V. Zakhava (1964; second edition, 1969). *The Word in an Actor's Art*, by M. O. Knebel (1964). *Traditions of Realism on Stage*, by Y. S. Kalashnikov (1964). *On the Art of the Theater*, by Yuri Zavadski (1965). *The Truth of the Theater*, by P. Markov (1965). *The Aesthetic Ideal of K. S. Stanislavski*, by Y. S. Kalashnikov (1965). *William Shakespeare, Our Contemporary*, by Grigori Kosintzev (1966). *Shakespeare in the Soviet Union* (collection of articles, 1966). *The Nemirovich-Danchenko School of Directing*, by M. O. Knebel (1966). *The Art of the Word*, by N. K. Gey (1967). *Soviet Film Actors* (collection of articles, 1968). *The Training of an Actor in the Stanislavski School of Acting*, by Grigori V. Kristi (1968). *The Key to the Character*, by Y. Smirnoff-Nesvitski (1970). *From Studio to Theater*, by L. Shikmatov (1970). *Drama As an Aesthetic Problem*, by A. A. Kariagin (1971). *The Life and Creativity of K. S. Stanislavski: Annals*, by I. Vinogradskaya (two volumes, 1971). *The History of Soviet Dramatic Theater* (six volumes, 1966–1971). *Directing as Practical Psychology*, by P. M. Ershov, forewords by Oleg Efremov and P. V. Simonov (1972).

Also, *Theater*, monthly publication of the Union of Writers of the USSR and the Ministry of Culture of the USSR (1963–1973).

The Stanislavski System

There is no Stanislavski System. There is only the authentic, incontestable one—the system of nature itself.

Artists who do not go forward go backward.

STANISLAVSKI

The difficult must become habit, habit easy, and the easy beautiful.

PRINCE SERGEI VOLKONSKI

The System cannot be learned by heart; it has to be assimilated, absorbed gradually. To know the System means to be able to use it; it must be learned as an unbreakable whole, without dividing its various elements. Isolated study of the elements can fragment the actor's behavior on stage.

Stanislavski
and His System

*Art establishes the basic human truths which
must serve as the touchstones of our judgment.
. . . I look forward to an America which will
steadily raise the standards of artistic accomplish-
ment and which will steadily enlarge cultural
opportunities for all of our citizens.*

PRESIDENT JOHN F. KENNEDY
Address at Amherst College, October 1963

We have many talented young people who want to
be in the theater. The mastery of professional technique can transform them into artists. It is time we
thought about our own tradition, and how it will
encourage our theater to flourish. President Kennedy's
views about art echoed those of Konstantin Sergeye-
vich Stanislavski, the great Russian actor, director, and
reformer of the theater. For Stanislavski, theater was
an institution of cultural and moral education. Theater,
he believed, besides being entertainment, should develop people's taste and raise the level of their culture.
To serve such theater should be an actor's super-super-
objective, he said. With this principle Stanislavski
expressed the aesthetic and ethical goals of theater art.

"Theater," said Stanislavski, "is a pulpit which is the
most powerful means of influence." "With the same
power with which theater can ennoble the spectators

3

it may corrupt them, degrade them, spoil their taste, lower their passions, offend beauty." "My task is to elevate the family of artists from the ignorant, the half-educated, and the profiteers, and to convey to the younger generation that an actor is the priest of beauty and truth." "Some actors and actresses love stage and art as fish love water," he wrote in his notebook. "They revive in the atmosphere of art. Others love not art itself but an actor's career, success; they revive in the backstage atmosphere. The first are beautiful, the others are abominable." "The habit of being always in public, of exhibiting oneself and showing off, of receiving applause, good reviews, and so on, is a great temptation; it accustoms an actor to being worshiped; it spoils him. His little ambitious person begins to need constant tickling." "To be content with such interests, one must be mediocre and vulgar. A serious artist cannot be satisfied for long with such existence, but superficial people are enslaved by the temptations of the stage, and become corrupted. This is why, in our work more than in any other, one must constantly keep oneself in hand. An actor needs a soldier's discipline." Without compromise or exception and without mercy, Stanislavski imposed such discipline. "I consider good manners as part of an actor's creativity," he said. He also remarked, "If you must spit, learn to do it before you enter the theater."

Believing ethics to be of great significance in the success of the theater, Stanislavski said that even very talented actors should be sacrificed if they could not contribute to the harmonious atmosphere of the group. Since the art of the theater is collective work, it is essential that everyone in the group work for the benefit of the whole performance and not solely for himself. Ethics, high morale, and stern discipline are indispensable in such a group. The reproduction of life on stage is, for actors, both a challenge and a responsibility toward the people who come to see it. An actor's exciting profession is one of responsibility, because it is he who breathes life into a written play, he who makes the play tangible, alive, valid, and exciting. "The theater infects the audience with its noble ecstasy," said Stanislavski.

Ethics impregnate all Stanislavski's teachings and are indivisible from his technology. He believed that an actor without ethics is only a craftsman, and without professional technique he is a dilettante. Ethics, profound knowledge, and a highly artistic form of expression are the essence of the Stanislavski System.

It became Stanislavski's goal to give an actor control over the phenomenon of inspiration. When an actor is inspired he is in the same natural and spontaneous state that is ours in life, and he lives the experiences and emotions of the character he portrays. In such a state, Stanislavski thought, an actor has the greatest power to affect the minds and feelings of his audience. Stanislavski's aesthetic and ethical beliefs formed the point of departure in his work and the driving force in the creation of his System.

I was quite young when I won a highly competitive entrance examination to the Third Studio of the Moscow Art Theater, which was guided and directed by Stanislavski's most celebrated disciple, the brilliant

Eugene B. Vakhtangov. Stanislavski said that Vakhtangov taught the technique better than he did himself; in fact, he was sometimes coached by Vakhtangov. To see such masters at work was truly thrilling. Each one's inexhaustible creative source was miraculous; both were unconditionally and tirelessly demanding of themselves and of others in achieving truth on the stage and in creating real characters. Never satisfied, Stanislavski and Vakhtangov were continually striving for better results.

It was understood that everyone in the Moscow Art Theater and its Studios would be present at rehearsals, whether actually involved in them or not. Since Vakhtangov appeared every night in a performance, he came to our Studio after eleven p.m., and our rehearsals continued until eight in the morning. Even in my early years I was interested in directing, and during the years I was in the Studio I never missed one of those rehearsals. Blessed with the gifts of exceptional imagination and impetuous artistic temperament, Stanislavski and Vakhtangov often stimulated the actors by including themselves as characters in a rehearsal.

When our Studio played *Turandot* in the Moscow Art Theater itself, Stanislavski came backstage for the express purpose of encouraging the young actors and actresses. The excitement created by his majestic presence was tremendous.

Having first studied the System in the Studio and later having closely analyzed his teachings, I want to try to clarify what Stanislavski achieved with his indomitable logic, his sensitive observation, his serious attitude toward actors, and his love of the theater. Because his scientific and artistic teachings about the creative state on stage are vital for good theater, and because he wanted simple books on acting technique, I wish to bring the knowledge of his teachings up to date in the United States.

One cause of misunderstanding about the Stanislavski System is the fact that various disciples of Stanislavski were assimilating it during different stages of its formation; without realizing that the System underwent constant change in its development, they could not find a common language, and their disagreement provoked confusion among those who had not been in touch with Stanislavski. Another cause is the insufficiency of material in English about Stanislavski's conclusions and deductions. The Stanislavski System is the science of theater art. As a science it does not stand still; being a science, it has unlimited possibilities for experiment and discoveries. Elements of the System have continually evolved and been tested, much as new chemicals are tested in a laboratory.

Before Stanislavski was born in 1863, Mikhail Shchepkin (1788–1863) had already fought against the artificial, declamatory style. This great actor of the Imperial Maly Theater was called "the father of realism" because he was the first to introduce truthful and realistic acting into the Russian theater. Stanislavski, impressed by Shchepkin's teachings and by his brilliant disciple, the actress Glikeria Fedotova, began to work on a technique which would enable an actor to build a live human being on the stage. Stanislavski's concepts were also greatly influenced by the plays of Anton Chekhov. The names of these two masters, along with that of the playwright and director Vladimir Ivanovich Nemirovich-Danchenko, became inseparable from the Moscow Art Theater. Chekhov wrote truthfully about ordinary men and women; he searched for the inner beauty in people and exposed their triviality and vice. Under Shchepkin's and Chekhov's influence Stanislavski strove to create an artistically conceived image of life on the stage.

The System has been found vitally important not only for beginners but also for experienced actors. Stanislavski proved that an actor with great talent and subtle nuances needs more technique than others, and thus emphasized his rejection of the widespread layman's opinion that a gifted actor does not need any technique at all.

Simplicity and scenic truth became important principles, and the Stanislavski System emerged as a vigorous weapon against overacting, clichés, and mannerisms. The System has become a creative technique for the truest portrayal of characters in any play, comedy or tragedy, whether by Chekhov or Ibsen, Shakespeare or O'Neill. The System has been recognized as a revolutionary theatrical development and is used throughout Russia, even by actors of theaters with tendencies entirely different from those of the Moscow Art Theater.

The Stanislavski System, destined to play an outstanding role in the development of twentieth-century theater, came to birth through Stanislavski's dedicated search over forty years for the answers to problems of actors and directors and for laws of creativeness. Nowhere in the world of theater can directorial or acting problems be solved without taking Stanislavski's teachings into consideration. With the System's terminology—super-objective, logic of actions, given circumstances, communion, subtext, images, tempo-rhythm, and so on—a common language has been created.

Stanislavski discovered and formulated laws but did not have time to develop them fully. Though the System's scientific, aesthetic, and ethical foundation cannot be changed, it can be further developed.

Since Stanislavski's death his teachings have been subject to analysis and study by important actors, directors, scholars, and scientists. Through the efforts of these experts to preserve the Stanislavski teachings for world theater, the System became more concrete and some of its more complicated demands easier to realize. Their deductions are important not only for actors and directors—for whom Stanislavski was creating his System—but also for dramatists and even scientists. "Theater and dramaturgy are one whole," said Stanislavski. "Only as a result of two arts—that of the dramatist and that of the theatrical group—will the new value, the performance, be born."

Before Stanislavski, drama schools everywhere in the world taught only the physical elements of an actor's training: ballet, fencing, voice, speech, diction, the importance of which we shall discuss further. There was no *inner acting technique*. The historical significance of Stanislavski lies in his discovery of laws for an actor's creativeness and his development of the first theory of theater art.

Theater experts throughout the world agree that it is the actors capable of discovering the inner life of the man they portray, actors capable of building "the life of the human spirit," as Stanislavski called it, who will lead the theater to progress. Not through specially built stages and auditoriums, not even through directors' inventions, but through actors capable of creating ever-new human beings, with their own unique inner worlds, will theater advance. Facing again and again a new personality, participating in all that happens around it, presents inexhaustible possibilities for an actor.

"Artists of colors, sounds, chisels, and words choose their art in order to communicate through their works with other people," wrote Stanislavski. Therefore the goal of art is spiritual communication with people. The inner creative process must be conveyed to the audience. "The most important thing is to build the life of the human spirit," Stanislavski said, and he developed a technique with the help of which actors can build the soul of a role, the inner world of the person created on the stage.

Stanislavski's teachings are not the result of personal guesswork: they form a science based on human functioning according to laws of nature. These laws are obligatory for all people. The title that Stanislavski gave to his System—"The Elementary Grammar of Dramatic Art"—emphasizes the universality of the laws for any actor building any character in any play.

"What I write does not refer to one epoch and its people, but to the organic nature of artists of all nationalities and of all epochs," he said. The System therefore cannot be called a Russian phenomenon, and does not have to be "adapted" to American actors or to actors of any nationality. Through the System, actors learn natural laws and how to use them consciously in re-creating human behavior on stage.

Thanks to his contact with the great scientist Ivan Petrovich Pavlov (1849–1936), whose teachings about conditioned reflexes became important in the same era as Stanislavski's own teachings, the reformer of the theater had an opportunity to study neurophysiology and to give scientific foundation to his System. Even scientists were astounded by his discoveries.

Stanislavski saw that (probably because of the artificial atmosphere of the stage) in front of a mass of people an actor's senses are often prone to paralysis. The actor then loses the feeling of real life and forgets how to do the simplest things that he does naturally and spontaneously in life. Stanislavski realized that an actor has to learn anew to see and not just to pretend to see, to hear and not just to pretend to listen, that he has to talk to his fellow actors and not just to read lines, that he has to think and to feel.

Stanislavski knew that an actor's mind, will, and emotions—the three forces responsible for our psychological life—must participate in the creation of a live human being on stage. In the evocation of emotions Stanislavski faced a difficult problem. He discovered that there are mechanisms in human beings which are not ordinarily subordinate to our control. For instance, we cannot at will slow our heart's palpitation or dilate blood vessels as easily as we can close our eyes or raise a hand, nor can an actor who comes on stage with no personal reason for experiencing emotions of fear, compassion, joy, or grief command them, because emotional reactions also belong to such uncontrolled mechanisms.

To these inner mechanisms Stanislavski gave the name *subconscious*. The problem seemed to him insoluble until, while watching great actors, he became aware that an actor, although he has no real reason to suffer or to rejoice on stage, begins to have true emotions when he is inspired. This fact brought Stanislavski to the idea that the *subconscious*—the uncontrolled complex of emotions—is not altogether unapproachable, and that there must be a kind of key which would intentionally "turn on" this inner mechanism. He began studying the possibility of deliberately arousing emotions, of indirectly influencing the psychological mechanism responsible for the emotional state of a human being.

During his many years of searching, Stanislavski experimented with various "conscious means to the subconscious." Each of these—including the forcing of emotions, so popular among American actors—though progressive at the time, brought Stanislavski disappointment until he developed his "method of physical actions," which he called the key to the emotional reactions of an actor, the basis of an actor's creativity, the essence of the whole System, and his creative heritage of the theater. *"The method of physical actions,"* said Stanislavski, *"is the result of my whole life's work."*

Thus Stanislavski found the "conscious means to the subconscious," which he had been seeking for over forty years. (A detailed explanation of the method of physical actions is given in the chapter that follows.) Though it was at the end of his career that Stanislavski gave the name to this key to the subconscious, it was not a late addition to his System. His teachings on action impregnate the whole technique from beginning to end; it is the leitmotiv of the whole System. The more fully Stanislavski understood human behavior, which he called "action," the more the System progressed. Since science has confirmed that the method of physical actions is based on physiological law, an actor's creative state (when his whole psycho-physical apparatus is involved) depends on it and cannot be neglected. With it, Stanislavski *reversed* the use of means by which he tried to bring an actor into a creative state. He realized that an experience before the actor's entrance could occur only by accident. Now the actor goes on stage to fulfill simple physical actions without forcing an experience beforehand. In fulfilling the unique physical action, the actor involves the psychological side of the action by reflex; this includes emotions.

The Stanislavski terms "conscious" and "subconscious" are really "controlled" and "uncontrolled." The actor's work is not a subconscious process. The Stanislavski System does not allow an actor to be subject to accidental intuition. In fact, conscious activity has the leading role in the System. But after an actor has consciously prepared the pattern of his role and approaches the play's events as if they were happening for the first time (following Stanislavski's formula, "today, here, now," which makes every performance different), his contact with the audience may give birth to true, spontaneous actions that are unexpected even by the actor himself. These are moments of "subconscious" creativity when an actor *improvises* although his text and the pattern of his role are firmly fixed. Such creativity or inspirational improvisation is the goal and essence of the Stanislavski school of acting. All Stanislavski's searchings were directed to finding means to "harness" this phenomenon and to subordinate it to an actor's conscious control. Actors are rarely aware of these moments of subconscious creativity and have difficulty in keeping them; the moments die if an actor tries to repeat them mechanically. Theater, being an artistic re-creation of life, according to Stanislavski, shares one of life's great problems: the moments passed on the stage cannot be repeated, as spent moments in real life cannot be brought back. When actors try to repeat what they did the night before, the theater stops being art because it stops being alive. Every performance in a living theater is as different as each day is different, and in order that the theater should be alive, there must be living people on the stage.

Stanislavski determined the favorable conditions for subconscious activity, or improvisation due to inspiration, which is the goal of an actor's art. We find that it is born through the conscious effort of the actor who has mastered his technique. Inspiration is the *result* of conscious hard work; it is not a power that stimulates work. As Stanislavski said, "There are no accidents in art—only the fruits of long labor."

The first scientific book to make an analysis of the Stanislavski System from the point of view of neurophysiology is entitled *The Method of K. S. Stanislavski and the Physiology of Emotions* by P. V. Simonov, prominent physiologist and member of the Academy of Science of the USSR. Simonov does not believe that an actor must study physiology in order to act convincingly; the important fact is that physiology has scientifically proved the correctness of the Stanislavski System. Not to study the Stanislavski System, says Simonov, is as dangerous for actors as it is dangerous for writers not to study the rules of language. Simonov, however, warns that he is attempting not to teach actors but to learn from Stanislavski for his own field.

Russian scientists, helped by important theater experts, have found in the Stanislavski System an invaluable source of observation concerning physiology and the problems of controlled and uncontrolled reactions. They realize that the Stanislavski motto "Subconscious through conscious means" has a direct connection with actual problems of human neurophysiology. Simonov says, "Modern rational psychotherapy does not have at its disposal the concrete means of conscious influence on neuroses which cannot be influenced by direct effort of will. . . . The more is our loss, because a system of such means exists; it has been thoroughly developed and checked a thousand times in practice. The system we have in mind is Stanislavski's 'method of physical actions.'" In his analysis, Simonov concludes that it is indisputable that the rules formulated by Stanislavski are the laws for an actor's creativity. And Simonov confirms the Stanislavski rule, "Emotions cannot be stirred directly."

Believing firmly that to build the life of a human spirit is *most* important in an actor's art, Stanislavski never tired of repeating that an actor must incarnate the behavior of the character to make it seen and heard—to be clear to the audience in every way. An actor with deficient speech or an untrained voice and body will not be able to convey the subtle nuances of inner life and will bore his audience. Stanislavski insisted on the continual polishing of an actor's physical apparatus. Stanislavski's belief about the incarnation of the inner life is in accord with what Leonardo da Vinci said to his disciples: "The soul does not like to be without its body because without the body it cannot feel or do anything; therefore build a figure in such a way that its pose tells what is in the soul of it." And Feodor Chaliapin, the great singer and actor, said, "A gesture is a movement not of a body but of a soul." Before Stanislavski, an actor's training consisted mainly of learning intonations and gestures. This resulted in artificial poses and flat declamations. But correcting this does not mean neglecting vividness of speech. "Every punctuation mark has its own intonation," Stanislavski said. "Treasure the spoken word." Through the Stanislavski technique actors learn to "enrich the ground," which makes their intonations expressive.

Stanislavski's demand for profound truth, simplicity, and naturalness does not mean merely an external presentation of naturalness. Stanislavski fought with determination the new cliché "naturalness," used by actors who did not understand him. His important demand, "Go from yourself," which we shall consider in the chapter "Work on the Role," has been sometimes oversimplified. Good theater is theater of profound thought and profound spiritual experience. In good theater an actor creates the inner experiences of the character, incarnates them, and makes this creative process understandable to the audience. Actors who play only themselves are absurd. A character is a new human being, born of the elements of the actor himself united with those of the character conceived by the playwright.

The apprehension of some people that the Stanislavski System will bring actors to "a level of uniformity" has no ground. The System, on the contrary, encourages the flourishing of the actor's individual traits. The laws for the organic behavior of all actors are the same, but each reincarnation will be different, and the personality of each actor will always stamp his stage creations with his own distinctive mark.

The Stanislavski System, besides presenting laws obligatory for every actor and every director, also offers a concrete method of work on a play and on a role. With it, an actor builds a live and typical character on the basis of the organic nature of a human being.

The System also prepares the actor for an *ensemble* —the logical, truthful, purposeful mutual behavior of all characters. Just as human behavior in life depends on relationships with other people, in an ensemble each role is conditioned by all roles. "Collective creativeness, on which our art is based, necessarily demands ensemble," said Stanislavski. "Those who violate it commit a crime . . . against the art which they serve."

The Stanislavski System is not a series of rules for staging a naturalistic play or any other play. These teachings are beyond the limits of one theatrical direction in their historical significance. Stanislavski believed not in naturalism, which presents the surface of life, but in realism, which is truth of content. The System, by "turning on" the subconscious mechanisms, helps an actor to live the experiences of a character as if they were his own. This is even more important in an unconventional production where sets, props, lights, and sounds do not help to convince the audience of events on stage.

Emotions are stirred in an actor in order to stir the spectator's emotions in turn. When an actor's emotions do not flow, his influence on the spectator weakens. Even the most imaginative directorial invention will be empty of sense if an actor's behavior on stage does not affect the spectators. There is no contradiction between unconventional staging and an actor who lives the inner experiences of the character. The sets and props do not have to be naturalistic. It is the truth of the actor's behavior that will keep the audience's attention. Though the means of expression will be different from those necessary for Chekhov, Gorki, or O'Neill, actors must also use Stanislavski's laws in tragedies by Shakespeare or Schiller and in plays by Brecht or Genet. If a director respects the dramatist, he will find the style of the play. Stanislavski encouraged any style of staging that a director found necessary to express the play in question. But he was against directors who were interested only in their own inventions, without respect for the author. "I salute every direction in our art," he said, "if only it helps correctly and artistically to transmit the life of the human spirit."

Though Stanislavski used to rehearse a play for several months, his technique, if properly understood and learned, will prove extremely useful in the American theater, where a play is rehearsed for only a few weeks. The System teaches an actor to work independently and therefore to accomplish what the director demands of him. In a theater where the director on occasion has time only to demand results, it is especially valuable to know how to achieve these quickly and effectively.

It is indisputable that there is a great deal of dilettantism in the theater, and Stanislavski fought it through the System. He considered even an accidental inspiration a form of dilettantism. His System teaches *professionalism*, and through professionalism theater becomes art. The widespread opinion that the actor's work is something mysterious which cannot be learned consciously was considered by Stanislavski to be a prejudice and, like all prejudices, harmful to culture and progress. Stanislavski regarded it as an alibi for an actor's laziness.

It is wrong to think that gifted actors never work.

Biographies of great actors prove the contrary; these artists searched constantly for a conscious technique, and worked on every inner and outer motion, on that mastery of every word which makes theater the strongest expression of the creative arts. All that is valuable in art is achieved through persistent work. The great Italian actress Eleonora Duse was known as a hard worker. Talma, the famous French actor of the eighteenth century, said that an actor needs twenty years to master his profession. And the celebrated nineteenth-century Russian actress Glikeria Fedotova said that actors were wasting their time waiting for the god Apollo to send them inspiration from heaven; Apollo was too busy with his own affairs, she said, and she advised actors to work hard to be able to evoke inspiration.

In other arts the audience sees the *result* of a creative process. In theater the audience is present *during* that process. Thus we cannot overemphasize how important it is for the actor to master his means of expression. Through the Stanislavski System actors learn to make conscious use of the laws of their organic nature; they learn their means of expression and become true professionals. The System teaches them to function on the stage automatically as live human beings. In mastering this technique, actors will not have to depend on chance. For chance, as every artist knows, is the enemy of art.

The Method
of Physical Actions

Stanislavski discovered that there is an unbreakable tie between the psychological and the physical in a human being. In every physical action there is always something psychological. For instance, opening a door is a physical action, but one always opens a door for some inner psychological reason. And in a psychological action there is always something physical: if you want to leave the room (this is psychological), you may go to the door (a physical action), and others will know that you intend to leave. Sometimes complete external immobility may be an expression of inner activity; upon hearing tragic news a person may remain physically still. There is no inner experience without external physical expression; it is with our bodies that we transmit to others our inner experiences. "The first fact," said Stanislavski, "is that the elements of the human soul and the particles of a human body are indivisible." The thesis of Stanislavski that the complex of a human's psychological life—moods, desires, feelings, intentions, ambitions, for example—is expressed through simple physical action has been confirmed by such scientists as Pavlov and I. M. Sechenov.

An actor's imagination is in constant conflict with real life: he faces his fellow actor or actress instead of a character in a play; instead of an ocean or a blue sky he sees a painted canvas; he comes to the theater with his own personal problems. No matter how fertile his imagination, the actor cannot honestly believe that he is the personality he portrays. But there is a level on which an actor finds coincidence between himself and the character. This is the level of physical actions. The only thing an actor can fulfill truthfully on stage as a character is a simple physical action. He can bang his fist on a table; he can slam the door; he can *ask* a question; he can *explain* something to his fellow actor; he can *threaten* or *encourage* him—and he can do all this truthfully. Stanislavski called these "physical actions." The *word*, said Stanislavski, is the physical side of the psychophysical process; images and the meanings behind the words form its psychological side. (For a detailed explanation of "verbal action," see the chapter "Work on the Role.")

Every character in a play performs definite actions in the circumstances given by the author. Executing these actions should become the actor's main problem. Stanislavski warned the actor not to try to "squeeze" emotions, but to act logically and truthfully. The more an actor forces an emotion, the less he is likely to stir it. In the sphere of physical actions everything is accessible to one's control; any of these actions can be executed and repeated many times, independently of an actor's mood.

Paths of nerves connect our physical actions with the inner mechanisms of emotions and of the innumerable nuances of human experience. The tangibility of these actions introduces the actor into the sphere of the character's life. The building of the character's logic of action is simultaneously the building of the logic and consecutiveness of emotions. Physical action is the "bait" for emotion, a pretext for involving the psychological life, said Stanislavski. *All attention* must be directed to the execution of physical actions, to their logical consecutiveness. Only truthful, concretely executed physical actions, indispensable in the given circumstances, involve true emotions. "The 'small truth' of physical actions stirs the 'great truth' of thoughts, emotions, experiences, and a 'small untruth' of physical actions gives birth to a 'great untruth' in the region of emotions, thoughts, and imagination," said Stanislavski. All the elements of the System, which were important in their own right at the time that he was developing them, are now intended to contribute to the truthful execution of physical action.

Human action, or behavior, which is a psychophysical process, is conditioned by environment. The circumstances created by the playwright add nuance and color to the scenic action. For instance, the action of opening a door to escape from a room will be different from opening it for the purpose of overhearing what is said in another room; it will be different if you open the door to let in somebody you love; it can be different if you open the door during the day or night; and so on. Consequently, an actor must know all the circumstances that condition each simple action. Because of the environment of a person, and the changing events around him, there cannot be two identical actions. A true psychophysical action, therefore, can never be a cliché. Clichés result from physical movements used without inner justification, without the knowledge of what has prompted them. Stanislavski abhorred all poses, gestures, and intonations which are the actor's aim, not the character's. He demanded the true, purposeful psychophysical action that comes when the movement is justified inwardly. He superseded the system of "expressive movement" formulated by François Delsarte (1811–1871), who suggested that an emotion could be expressed with a "prescribed" gesture, established beforehand. A human gesture depends on numerous factors, such as the individual's specific traits, the tempo-rhythm in which he acts at the given moment, and other circumstances.

There is just as much danger in an actor's preoccupation with the psychological side of the action, without necessary physical expression. Stanislavski said that an actor thus preoccupied *does not* actually execute the action, as it is a psychophysical process. An actor will achieve a creative state when his whole psychophysical apparatus is involved through his effort to fulfill the scenic action. This, in the words of the Polish director Jerzy Grotowski, is the "total act."

Exercises and Improvisations°

An analogous experience in your own life should be, as much as possible, the basis for the situation in any improvisation; it may be adapted. Before executing an improvisation, concentrate and build in your imagination the circumstances in which the action takes place, why you do it, where it takes place, when. Think of *all possible details* in each situation. Be yourself, though in different circumstances. In your imagination see persons you really know in life. After you have built the situation, find physical behavior that will project it. You will then be fulfilling the psychophysical action.

Most exercises should be done to music.

1 Sit, stand, walk. Justify everything you do. For example, sit at a window in order to see what is happening in the house opposite. Sit in order to rest.

2 Stand to be photographed. Stand in order to see better.

3 Walk to pass the time. Walk to annoy the people who live in the apartment below.

4 Clean your bureau drawers.

5 Count the number of objects on a table.

6 You have to leave school because you cannot afford to pay tuition. A friend wants to help you but she has no money. She brings you a valuable brooch. You refuse the gift but your friend insists, lays it on a

---

° The examples for exercises and improvisations in this text are not all Stanislavski's. He encouraged students of drama to invent their own. Exercises and improvisations are valid if they give the actor an awareness of the laws of nature by which we function in real life and if they teach psychophysical behavior on stage.

dresser, and leaves. You walk with your friend to the door. When you come back to the dresser, you find that the brooch has disappeared. Can anyone have taken it while you weren't looking?

7 Burn a letter. First, think why you do it. Think what you may have done in a real situation when you had to burn a letter.

In all exercises and improvisations the actor must think of three steps: beginning, development, and end. Think of your action, not of your feelings. You will feel at ease and relaxed if you concentrate on action. Do not try too hard, but do not be nonchalant or careless. Be concrete in what you do. Do not do anything "in general." " 'In general,' " said Stanislavski, "is the enemy of art."

"Purposefulness connects the simplest (physical) action with the most complex (psychological) action. This connection was discovered for the first time by Stanislavski as the objective nature of the actor's work, which from beginning to end, in its best and worst manifestations, is the art of action." (From P. M. Ershov's *Directing as Practical Psychology*.)

Elements
of an Action

The elements described in this section are important aids in carrying out the truthful, logical, concrete action; therefore the "turning on" of an actor's subconscious, so that he will create intuitively, subconsciously, depends on them.

The "Magic *If*"

Stanislavski did not think that an actor could honestly believe in the truth and reality of events on stage, but he said that an actor can believe in the possibility of events. An actor must only *try* to answer the question, "What would I do *if* I were in King Lear's position?" This "magic *if*," as Stanislavski called it, transforms the character's aim into the actor's. It is a strong stimulus to inner and physical actions.

If carries the actor into the imaginary circumstances. In asking, "What would I do *if* I were . . ." an actor does not have to force himself to believe that he is such a person in such circumstances. *If* is a supposition, and it does not imply or assert anything that exists. Through it an actor can create problems for himself, and his effort to solve them will lead him naturally to inner and external actions. *If* is a powerful stimulus to imagination, thought, and logical action. And, we have seen, a correctly executed logical action will stir the actor's inner mechanism of emotions.°

Improvisations

1 You are dressing for an important reception. What would you do if the lights suddenly went out?

2 You have made all the preparations to go on vacation (tickets, hotels, and so on). What would you do if someone at your office called and told you that you must postpone your trip? While building the circumstances, see in your mind real persons whom you know in life.

3 You are on a train going to an important conference. What would you do if you suddenly realized that you were on the wrong train? Do you know where you are going, whom you are going to see, what for? What if you were a king; a spy; a teacher?

° In 1931 Charlie Chaplin wrote in an article that he was using the "magic *if*" for all his creative work.

Given Circumstances

Given circumstances include the plot of the play, the epoch, the time and place of the action, the conditions of life, the director's and the actor's interpretation, the setting, the properties, lighting, sound effects—all that an actor encounters while he creates a role. A person's psychological and physical behavior is subject to the external influence of his environment, and an action makes clear what a certain character does in the given circumstances of the play and why he does it. The character is built with these actions in the given circumstances. The actor must become so familiar with the environment of the play that he becomes part of it. The nuances and the color of the action will depend on the circumstances which provoke it. Only after the actor has studied the play, the events, and the given circumstances will he be able to select the actions which will involve his emotions and other inner experiences.

Improvisations

1 Put on a clean shirt after a day's work in a mine. Take your time to build the imaginary circumstances. You may be going to a party, or there might have been a serious accident in the mine.

2 Pack to go on vacation.

3 Pack to leave for war. Think of people you know in real life whom you would leave behind. Think hard

and build the imaginary circumstances which could arise in real life.

4 Enter your apartment after a party.

Imagination

Since the imagination plays a dominant role in the actor's task of transforming the story of the play into an artistic, scenic reality, an actor must be sure that it functions properly. The imagination must be cultivated and developed; it must be alert, rich, and active. An actor must learn to think on any theme. He must observe people and their behavior, try to understand their mentality. He must be sure to notice what is around him. He must learn to compare. He must learn to dream and with his inner vision create scenes and take part in them.

A playwright rarely describes the past or the future of his characters, and often omits details of their present life. An actor must complete his character's biography in his mind from beginning to end, because knowing how the character grew up, what influenced his behavior, and what he expects his future to be will give more substance to the present life of the character and will give the actor a perspective and a feeling of movement in the role. If an actor does not fill in all these missing events and movements, the life he portrays will not be complete.

A rich imagination will also contribute when an actor interprets the lines and fills them with the meaning that lies behind—the "subtext." The lines of the author are dead until an actor analyzes and brings out the sense that the author intended. A simple phrase such as "I have a headache" may mean various things; the person who says it may be afraid that the headache is a symptom of a serious illness; he may want a pretext to go away; he may be hinting to guests who will not leave. The meaning, the thought, and the intention are all important—not simply the words. If an actor with the help of his imagination finds interesting meaning behind the words, his intonations also will be expressive and interesting. "Spectators come to the theater to hear the subtext," said Stanislavski. "They can read the text at home."

Every word and movement of an actor on stage must be the result of a well-functioning imagination. Everything you imagine must be precise and logical. Always know who you are, when your imaginary scene is happening, where, how, and what for. All this will help you to have a definite picture of an imaginary life. Creative imagination will help an actor to execute actions naturally and spontaneously—this is the key to his emotions.

Improvisations

1 In your mind, go through a walk from class to home. Imagine being at home cleaning your room. Follow your logic and closely watch the work of your imagination. You will gradually stop being an observer and merge with the "you" you are watching. You will

be in the state which Stanislavski calls "I am," which means "I live," "I exist."

2 Describe a person whom you have met recently and who impressed you. Try to guess his interests.

3 Look at a picture of an unknown person. Explain who this could be. Try to guess the person's profession, what his family is like, what his tastes are; learn to judge from his attire, eyes, hair, and so on. Look at a picture of a landscape; then close your eyes and tell of its mood and of everything you saw in minute detail. Repeat this exercise several times, gradually diminishing the time you allow for examining the picture.

4 In your imagination, travel around the world.

5 Quickly make up answers to the most unexpected questions.

6 You are a member of a scientific expedition. Your plane is out of order. Decide where the forced landing takes place. Use your imagination to develop this accident in the greatest possible detail.

Do not imagine anything vaguely. Use all possible concrete, consecutive details. Logic and proper sequence will make what you imagine real. As you work on a role, your words will become your own when you have your own vision, your own picture of the events and of the people. You have to achieve a continuous, logical chain of images in your mind, related to the given circumstances.

In trying to make decisions, you will be led to actions. And a truthful action is the "key" which turns on your emotions.

Concentration of Attention

Several decades ago, when actors of the Moscow Art Theater began to study the Stanislavski System, they would spend ten or fifteen minutes in complete silence in order to concentrate. A well-known actress used to put a shawl over her head, and no one dared to approach her lest he interfere with her "concentration." At that time, Stanislavski believed that concentration was the key to achieving the creative state on stage.

Following scientific laws, Stanislavski said that an actor must concentrate his attention on stage objects sufficiently attractive to offset the distracting factors beyond the stage. He must *not*, however, try to forget the audience. For the actor to try to force himself into believing that he is alone, that he does not see anybody or hear anything in the audience, would also be contradictory to the art of the theater. The audience is an important co-creator of the performance. But it is possible to be without fear, to feel at ease, to forget one's worries and everything that interferes with stage creativeness, and to achieve what Stanislavski called *public solitude.*° This is possible if an actor gives maximum attention to the physical action and to all that his imagination is able to build around it. A concrete thought and a concrete physical action will hold the actor's attention. Fully concentrated attention depends on the thorough execution of the physical action.

° Some distort public solitude into "private moments" which would have shocked Stanislavski.

On stage an actor has to learn anew to see, to hear, and to think, because in front of an audience his natural faculties are often prone to paralysis. Actors frequently only pretend that they see or hear or think. If an actor is to be a live human being on stage, his faculties must function as they do in life. An actor's eye that really sees attracts the spectator's attention and directs it where he wants. An actor's eye which does not see takes the spectator's attention away from the stage. An actor can make himself actually see anything on the stage—a vase, a picture, a book—by building around it some imaginary details which will make it attractive to him. The more an actor exercises his concentration, the sooner it will become automatic; finally, it will become second nature to him.

At the start of training, it is necessary to practice with an object nearby. The actor must examine it in every detail. He must be relaxed and not make too great an effort. It is his imagination, not his body, that must make the effort to see. There must be no physical tension while he is concentrating his attention on the object. Every action must be executed with the amount of concentration that it would require in life. An inexperienced actor always feels that he does not give enough. "Cut ninety-five per cent," said Stanislavski. An actor need not try to amuse the audience. If with the help of his imagination he sees the object and is interested in it, the audience will also be interested.

To facilitate concentration of attention on execution of physical actions Stanislavski introduced *circles of attention*. An actor must limit his attention to separate parts of the stage, which he establishes with the help of objects on stage.

A *small circle of attention* is a small area that includes the actor and, perhaps, a nearby table with a few things on it. The actor is the center of such a small area and can easily have his attention absorbed by the objects inside it.

The *medium circle of attention* is an area that may include several persons and groups of furniture. An actor should examine this gradually, not trying to take it all in at once.

The *large circle of attention* is everything an actor can see on stage. The larger the circle, the more difficult it is to keep the attention from dissipating.

When an actor feels that his attention is wandering, he should immediately direct it to a single object and concentrate on it. When he succeeds and surmounts the difficulty, he can redirect his attention—first to a small circle, then to a medium one, then to a large one.

As well as learning to concentrate on things he sees on the stage, an actor must learn to concentrate on sounds he hears and on objects in his mind. When an actor succeeds in concentrating, he is truly active inwardly and physically, and therefore "turns on" his mechanism of emotions.

Exercises and Improvisations

The Stanislavski System follows the laws of nature. In life, concentration is not isolated from the human act. Therefore, concentration should not be practiced separately from an action. Fulfill an action with adequate concentration. Always build the circumstances in which actions are fulfilled, possibly based on an analogous situation in your life. Know what you do, why you do it, where, when. . . .

1 Examine any object that is close. Notice its form, lines, color, and any other detail. Then, without looking at it, tell what you remember. Gradually cut down the time allowed for absorbing the object. Build the circumstances. Do the same with an object at a moderate distance; with one far away.

2 Listen to the sounds in the street in specific circumstances. Tell what you hear.

3 Concentrate on an object in given circumstances. Gradually direct your attention to the small, to the medium, and to the large circles of attention and then back to the object.

For a group:

4 Count together to thirty. Clap your hands once when a number includes or may be divided by three. Then repeat the exercise, but clap twice when a number includes five or may be divided by five. If the number may be divided by both three and five, clap three times. Do the same counting in turn.

5 All stand. Move the right arm forward, then up, out to the side, and down. Then do the same with both arms, but keep the left one movement behind the right. Then do the same while walking in a circle. After each movement, evoke an image in your mind of what you are doing and adjust your body. The body must express what you are doing.

6 Try to identify sounds behind you (someone sweeping the floor, putting a letter into an envelope, for example).

While the student actor is learning to fulfill a psycho-physical action, his concentration develops. Observe and concentrate on people and nature. Enrich your impressions with music, paintings, literature. Penetrate into another person's inner world. Try to understand the reasons for his behavior. Practice this in life and do it on stage.

Truth and Belief

Truth on stage is different from truth in life. In a play there are no true facts or events; everything is invention. To believe, on stage, does not mean that an actor must practice self-hypnosis or force himself to have hallucinations. An actor who believes that he really is King Lear is emotionally ill. Belief means that an actor treats things or persons as if they were what he wants the audience to believe they are. An actor knows that his fellow actor is not his father or an emperor, but he can treat him as his father or as an emperor. He can treat an object as if it were a fluttering bird. The ability of an actor to make his audience believe what he wants it to believe creates scenic truth. The moments in which he succeeds in this constitute art on stage.

If an actor while carrying out an action uses logical consecutiveness, justifies everything with the help of the "magic *if*," and thinks of the given circumstances, he will not overact and his behavior will be truthful. Without forcing himself, he will believe in what he is doing because he will be doing it as in real life. Physical actions without the help of any objects ("with air") develop an actor's concentration, imagination, feelings of truth and belief, feeling of the right measure. Such exercises teach an actor to achieve the maximum of truthfulness in his action. Stanislavski considered them as important as scales and vocalisms are for the pianist and the singer.

A well-executed physical action is especially important to an actor during tragic moments in a play. While concentration on an inner tragic action may lead him to overact and to force his emotions (and emotions are "afraid" of forcing), a truthfully executed simple physical action related to and justified by the given moment will involve his psychophysical apparatus and make his faculties function: his truthful emotions in the given circumstances will appear, and he will be introduced naturally into the inner experiences of the character he portrays.

When an actor brings everything he does to the maximum of truthfulness and feels as if he were doing it in real life, he enters a state of "I am," where he merges with his role. Even a small untruth in the execution of a physical action destroys the truth of the psychological life. Truthful execution of a small physical action helps an actor's belief in what takes place on stage.

But in trying to make his actions truthful, an actor must remember that there are varieties of truth. There is uninteresting truth as well as interesting or unusual truth. In executing his actions, inner and physical, an actor must always look for the unexpected and the true at the same time. His actions must be free from unattractive details. They must be real but in good taste. Actions will be impressive if they are unusual, different. To find such unusual forms of truth, an actor must see and watch, absorbing all possible impressions.

Improvisations

1 Treat a chair as a vicious dog; as a throne; as a seat in a space ship.

2 Drink a liquid as a poison; as a cocktail; as hot tea.

3 Find a hidden object; then repeat your search after you know where it is hidden.

4 Stab yourself with a letter opener. Treat it as if it were a dagger.

Without objects:

5 Put a sheet of paper into an envelope. Thread a needle. Raise a pail full of water; raise an empty pail. Put a book on a shelf.

6 Dress for work. Take time to concentrate on building the given circumstances.

7 Dress for a party. Do it concretely. Use consecutive details.

8 Undress in a hospital; at home.

Special attention must be given to the size, shape, and weight of imaginary objects. Do these exercises at home with real objects, watching carefully the movements and positions of your body, hands, fingers.

To make those who watch you believe in what you are doing, you must achieve perfection in your actions. The exercises will teach you to do every physical action precisely, clearly, and logically.

Communion

To make the meaning and logic of his actions understandable to the spectators, an actor must communicate with them indirectly, through his communion with other actors. Stanislavski showed that (except in special cases, such as *commedia dell'arte*) when an actor has direct contact with spectators he becomes merely a reporter instead of a live character. This relationship disrupts the truth of the performance and distracts the audience from the play itself. An honest, unbroken communion between actors, on the other hand, holds the spectators' attention and makes them part of what takes place on stage.

The actor must be in communion with his real partner, not with an imaginary person. As our behavior in life depends on people around us, the actor's behavior as a character is related to that of the people around him; he has different relationships with those, for instance, who are friendly and with those who are hostile. His use of the "magic *if*" and of his imagination will help him to develop the proper attitudes toward each of his fellow actors. The actor depends upon the onstage events—conflicts, sympathies, antipathies, and other relationships among the characters; these events happen through the efforts of the entire group.

To be in communion with another person on stage means to be aware of that person's presence, to make sure that he hears and understands what you tell him and that you hear and understand what he tells you. That means mutual influence. Just as in life we see images before we speak, the actor, in order to influence his audience, must see images and transmit them to his fellow actors, and through active transmission of his lines an actor will impress on his fellow actor what he wants him to see and to hear. If he knows his action and energetically communicates it to the other actor, he will be "carried away" by the experience of the character he portrays. If he communicates with determination even to a bad actor, the other will respond. An actor must absorb what other persons tell him; their words, actions, and thoughts must come to him as if he were hearing them for the first time. During a dialogue, thoughts, projects, memories, or decisions must flow through the minds of the one who talks and of the one who listens. Their reactions must be physical and psychological and should not be interrupted when another actor speaks, or during silences and pauses. If an actor, while trying to influence his partner, strives to obtain a definite physical result (for instance, a smile), his aim becomes concrete; his imagination will be stirred and his attention concentrated, and he will achieve a strong communion.

But sometimes an actor talks to himself on stage. A monologue is a concentrated process of thinking aloud, expressing the character's mood—his thoughts and feelings. Without offering this as a part of his System, Stanislavski described how he himself behaved in order to be in communion with *himself*. He made the brain and the solar plexus, which are two centers of our nerves' life, "talk" to each other. He felt as if he had two I's which established a steady dialogue between themselves as if they were two actors.

To communicate with an imaginary object (for instance, the ghost of Hamlet's father), an actor must use the "magic *if*," telling himself honestly what he would do *if* he saw a ghost. The actor can also influence the audience through his contact with objects on stage, of which he must be properly aware.

An actor should not practice a dialogue without another person; otherwise he can become accustomed to receiving no reaction and might have difficulty in communicating on stage with a person who does react. An actor must learn to respond to his fellow actor, for it is what happens between the characters that is important and interesting to the audience. True communion takes place when a slight change in intonation of one evokes a change in intonation in another; change in the expression of a face of one will provoke change in another. Intonation, movement, and gesture are valuable if they arise from communion with the partner.

In mass scenes an actor may communicate with various people in the crowd. He may be in communion with one person or with all of them. Stanislavski demanded from each actor—not only the principals but even those who took part only in the mass scenes—a detailed biography of the character he was portraying. Actors without a single word to say created characters full of inner content and brought individual life to the stage.

The actor must make sharp use of his senses in order to achieve a strong sense of communion. When an actor without any physical tension sees intensely, hears intensely, and so on, he has a complete "grasp," as Stanislavski called it.

Improvisations

1 Two persons are sitting in an opera house listening to a performance. A person next to them finds that one of his neighbors is familiar to him. Trying to remember where he could have met this person, he disturbs the others. Think of real parties, or other places, of people you know in real life. Be aware of each other's behavior and react to it as you would in life, in a psychophysical way.

2 Two secret agents meet in a public place (a restaurant, an airport, etc.), and one has to hand the other an important document. There is a detective in the same place watching them. Try to pass over the document without being caught. You must attract your partner's attention. Be sure that he understands you and that you react appropriately to his behavior.

Evaluate your partner; make certain that you succeed in transmitting your images to him. Use your body.

Adaptation

An *adaptation*, or adjustment, is really the overcoming of a physical obstacle in achieving an aim. Once the actor has his aim in mind, and has evaluated the qualities of the person with whom he has to deal, he will think of an adaptation. To execute an action which answers "What do I do?" and "Why do I do it?" an actor will use various adaptations. An adaptation answers the question "How do I do it?" All three—"What?" "Why?" and "How?" (action, aim, and adaptation)—are parts of the scenic task. While the action and the aim may be determined beforehand, the adaptation will depend on the partner's behavior and on other obstacles that are encountered. In life we may know beforehand what we want to ask another person and why we want to do it, but how we do it often comes unexpectedly. Adaptations must be sought in the process of executing an action.

Adaptation is an especially effective means of communion between actors on the stage. To adjust oneself to another, one must be well aware of that person's presence and personality. For example: you have an important appointment at five o'clock. It is four forty-five and your employer is still dictating to you in his office. The necessity for evaluating the circumstances in relation to your employer, for inventing an ingenious reason to leave and to be on time for your appointment, requires you to find an adjustment for the situation and to overcome the obstacle to your aim.

Actors must adjust to one another on the stage, as

people in life do when they meet. A human being's behavior depends on his relationship with people around him: this law must be the basis of every scenic action. If you talk to a stupid person, you will try to adjust to his mentality and talk in a simple way so that he can understand you. If you are with a shrewd person, you have to act cautiously and look for subtle adaptations so that he does not see through you and does not guess what you have on your mind.

New conditions of life, a new atmosphere, a new place, the time of day or night—all require appropriate adaptation. People behave differently at night and during the day. In a foreign country one adjusts oneself to local conditions. The quality and variety of adaptation are extremely important on stage. To be interesting, an adaptation must be imaginative, in good taste, strong, and sharp.

Contrasting and unexpected adaptations are impressive. If, according to what is happening on stage, the audience expects an actor to scream at another actor, but instead of screaming he speaks softly, the effect can be very strong. If such an idea comes to an actor during a performance because he realizes suddenly that he will accomplish more that way with the man with whom he is angry, it means that it has come intuitively, subconsciously—at a moment of inspiration. He must not, however, repeat it during his next performance without first analyzing and understanding what made him behave in such an unexpected manner. Once he finds the reason, he may use it as the stimulus to this behavior every time he performs the same role.

Adaptations should not be transformed into an aim

of intentional effect on the audience, lest the truthfulness and logic of physical actions be disturbed and the actor be led to performing tricks for the spectactors' amusement. Adaptations should be logical in terms of the play's given circumstances. Too much preoccupation with *how,* before the actor knows what he is doing and why, leads to superficial adaptations.

When an actor fulfills truthfully a logical concrete action he achieves involvement of his psychophysical apparatus, his faculties function, and his inner mechanism of emotional reactions is involved. During such a creative process he may have brilliant ideas for adaptations which will come intuitively, subconsciously. But whether the actor observes an adaptation in life which he considers characteristic of his role or receives a suggestion for one from his director, he should bring it to the stage only after he has made it his own.

Improvisations

Before choosing actions, build the circumstances.

1 You want a favor of the person you meet for lunch. Try to achieve your purpose by means which would be most effective in the case. Take your time to build all the possible circumstances in which this could happen.

2 Your children will return home from school at any minute. You do not want them to notice the effect of tragic news on you.

3 You meet a man you were trying to avoid because

you owe him an explanation. What will you do? Everything you imagine must be logical and concrete. Use all possible adaptations to achieve your aim.

4 Meet a person you do not know.

5 Take leave of an important person.

Tempo-Rhythm

Tempo-rhythm is an important condition for concreteness and truthfulness in the execution of physical actions. During every minute of life there are tempo (speed) and rhythm (varying intensity of experience) within us as well as outside us. Every movement, every fact or event takes place in a corresponding tempo-rhythm. We go to work and come home in different tempo-rhythms. There are different tempo-rhythms inside us when we listen to music and when we listen to a fire siren. We also look at a beautiful landscape and at a traffic accident in different tempo-rhythms. Every action on stage must be executed in the tempo-rhythm required in life.

According to physiological laws, the correct tempo-rhythm contributes to concentration and consequently keeps the actor's attention from distracting factors. It plays an important role in mastering the logic and consecutiveness of actions.

Tempo-rhythm must correspond to the given circumstances. An actor cannot act sluggishly when energy is necessary. The truthfulness of actions will be lost, even when they are logical, if they are too slow or too fast.

The building of struggles in a role influences the rhythmic pattern. The rhythm changes when the objects of a struggle change, and different means are used in the struggle. Tempo-rhythm reflects the degree of inner involvement and depends on physical readiness to fulfill an action.

There is an individual right rhythm in every person. An actor must find it for the character he portrays. It will help him to feel correct in his role, and it is as important to him to find it as it is for a director to find the right rhythm for a whole performance.

Correct tempo-rhythm, by helping to make the action truthful, helps to stir the actor's emotions. It creates communion and ensemble work. Rhythm is a bridge between the inner experience and its physical expression. The wrong tempo-rhythm in one actor unbalances the other actors, and the audience then does not believe in what they say or do.

Exercises and Improvisations

1 You are having breakfast and you are late for work. Find the correct tempo-rhythm.

2 Write a letter to a person you love and write one to a creditor. Find a correct tempo-rhythm for each.

3 Move with music. Justify inwardly the different tempo-rhythms.

Emotional Memory

Stanislavski was constantly trying to increase his knowledge of all facets of man's inner life. He studied psychology, physiology, and aesthetics as well as historical and theoretical writing on the theater. He conferred with scientists and intellectuals in various specialized fields, and was especially interested in the works of the French psychologist Théodule-Armand Ribot (1839–1916), whose term "affective memory" he used. Later, in the 1930s, he rejected this name and replaced it with "emotional memory."

An experience of the actor on stage is different from an experience in life. The difference lies in the fact that the actor lives on stage as the character and also as the actor who creates the character. The experiences of the actor-character influence one another and acquire a specific quality. The actor's own experience, transformed into that of the character, is as sincere and deep on stage as in life. The quality of the actor's performance depends upon the sincerity of his experience. And yet the quality of the experience on stage changes, as Stanislavski said, into a "poetic reflection of life's experience." He said, "Time is an excellent filter, an excellent purifier of memories of emotions once experienced. Moreover, time is an excellent artist. It not only purifies but is capable of poeticizing the memories."

The actor must live true experiences, but true *stage* experiences. The actor on stage lives a "repeated" experience, not a "primary" one, as Stanislavski said.

Every actor knows the difference between a real-life experience and an experience on stage if he ever achieves an experience on stage. Indeed, if actors lived the same experiences as in life, there would be lunatics and murders on stage after every performance in which a character loses his mind or a murder is committed. It would be impossible for an actor to survive many performances in which he went through experiences and shocks as they are in real life. On the contrary, we know that suffering on stage gives the actor who achieves it a true joy.

It should be obvious, therefore, that a stage emotion is not the same as an emotion in life, first of all because it does not arise from an actual cause. The actor is capable of stirring a needed emotion within himself only because he has often experienced an analogous emotion in his own life. Every experience in life leaves a trace on our central nervous system, and thus the nerves which participate in a given experience become more sensitive to such a stimulus. Every adult has experienced most emotions, though perhaps not for exactly the same reason the actor must experience them on stage. People may go through different feelings of love, for instance: love for a person, a dress, an animal, sunshine. We have also hated someone, or an insect, or war. There is something common in all these cases: that is why they are all called love and hate.

According to scientific data, emotional memory not only retains an imprint of an experience but also synthesizes feelings of a different nature. If a person has experienced, for instance, the feeling of envy because his friend has a better job, or wins a lottery, or receives a good role in a play, and if he has experienced such feelings many times, the common element in all these cases will have left a deep imprint on his memory. Stanislavski said, "From many preserved traces of what was experienced, one great condensed, magnified, and deepened memory of emotions of the same nature is formed. There is nothing superfluous in such a memory; there is only the essence. This is the synthesis of all the emotions of the same kind. It does not refer to a small, separate, private instance, but to all those of the same nature." The actor must be capable of bringing out the imprint of a past experience and of making it respond to the conditioned stimulus on stage at the moment he needs it. Through rehearsals, the actor develops a conditioned reflex in which his emotion is stirred through the stage stimulus.

A re-created emotion is different from the "primary" emotion also because it does not absorb the actor entirely. Reliving a real-life experience, the person also lives the present time, and this influences the experience. When a tragedy occurs, we are completely absorbed in the moment, but when we remember this tragedy later, other interests penetrate the experience. Though our grief is sincere, it acquires a different quality. Such is the actor's state on stage. The actor who sincerely lives the life of the character never forgets that he is the actor who performs.

Stanislavski believed in two sources of material for an actor's creative work: the inner life of an actor himself and his observations of the outside world—an inexhaustible source. The material an actor finds in the life around him he must make his own. To enrich the emotional memory, the actor must observe what is happening around him; he must read, listen to music, go to museums, watch people. Well-developed emotional memory is the most important requirement for the actor's work in the theater of living experience. It is the storage of past experiences and the *only* source for emotions on stage.

In the early stages of the System, actors tried to bring themselves into the creative state when their emotions were stirred, with the help of its separate elements. But that state would not always come, and they were "acting" their emotions. Moreover, Stanislavski felt that forcing emotions from the emotional memory brought actors to inner hysteria. Stanislavski feared that such a tendency could ruin the actor's mental health and art. Experience also showed that isolated study and use of the elements of the System dismembered the System into separate parts which were later difficult to reassemble into one whole. Students may be virtuosos on exercises in "concentration," "relaxation," or "without objects" but remain unable to fulfill an action that includes these organic elements. Thus the principal objective of the System— involvement of the psychophysical apparatus of the actor when his emotions are stirred—is not achieved.

With his method of physical actions Stanislavski revolutionized the use of means by which an actor achieves the creative state. Emotional memory stores our past experiences; to relive them, actors must execute indispensable, logical physical actions in the given circumstances. There are as many different nuances of emotions as there are different physical actions.

Starting rehearsals of Molière's *Tartuffe* on the basis of the final developments of his System, Stanislavski said to the members of the Moscow Art Theater, "I am not going to live long.° It is my duty to transmit to actors my experience and my knowledge. Learn to carry out correctly and organically the simplest physical actions. The logic and consecutiveness of these actions will evoke in you the entire complicated, subtle scale of inner experiences. Carrying out the logic of a physical action will bring you to the logic of emotions, and this is everything for an actor."

° Rehearsals of *Tartuffe* were interrupted by Stanislavski's death.

Analysis through
Events and Actions

Actors must project the main idea of the play. Since it is much easier to understand an immediate purpose than a distant one, the long-range aim will be discovered through important events, the consecutive actions revealing each event. By determining the actions, the actor is able to build a logical, consecutive performance and to assimilate his role—and this practice will also be exceptionally helpful to him in memorizing the part.

Every human action has a definite aim, and answers the question, "What do I do?" "Why do I do it?" and "How do I do it?" An actor must remember that his reason for being on stage is to convey what he does and why he does it at a given moment.

Stanislavski recommended beginning the analysis of a play with the determination of events, or, as he said, the "active facts," which dictate the actions. It is essential to understand the important events and not to dwell on secondary ones. Important events lie at the root of a good play and move its action as well as that of each character. Determination of those events involves the circumstances and is the shortest way to the understanding of the play.

Each event has a main action; for example, a friend comes to help a married couple to settle a difference. His main action is to *help*. In trying to help he may want to persuade the husband to pay more attention to his wife, he may *reproach* the woman for not being serious enough about her duties, and so on. By striving energetically to carry out these actions, which are really adaptations or means to achieve the aim, the actor reveals the event on stage.

While searching for a method of analysis which would fully disclose the essence of a play, Stanislavski for many years taught and applied the process of breaking up the play into its various episodes, analyzing and discovering the actions by having the director and the actors sit around a table with their scripts and pencils. He loved this preparatory period, which preceded rehearsals and which lasted a long time. In the last years of his directorial and pedagogical career, Stanislavski changed this practice. He said that these long sessions around the table led to serious errors because they divided spiritual and physical behavior. So Stanislavski started rehearsals almost immediately after discussing the main idea. Actors analyzed the events and investigated the psychophysical behavior of the characters on stage, *in action*.

In order to understand what his action is at a given

moment, an actor must analyze the essence of an event. Actions must be strongly related to the idea of the play. Everything an actor does on stage must contribute to this. If the actor fulfills his action, he will convey it to his audience; by being truly active in a psychophysical way he will involve his entire apparatus and his emotions will be stirred.

Every important event should be given a carefully selected name; it should not be a verb and should be so characteristic that the single term gives the actors the essence of the event. The name of the event is the same for all characters, but their reactions to it, and therefore their actions, will be different. As the actors and the director learn more about the play, they may change the names of some events.

To define an action an active verb should be used; it should express precisely and logically the end an actor wants to achieve. If, in the process of his work on a role, an actor feels that he should change the action, he must do so and change its name.

Determining the actions makes the character's behavior justified and purposeful. And as a result of understanding the actions, an actor will come to understand the subtext. In order really to understand the actions, an actor will have to analyze the play, the character, the epoch in which the play takes place, and other given circumstances. Not intuition alone, but the actor's penetration into the intention of the playwright, his ability to choose what is most typical for the character, will determine the correct definition of actions for the role. The necessity of verbally expressing the actions forces the actor to think and to study his role and the whole play.

There is usually something that opposes the action. An actor must find these obstacles which the character must try to overcome. For instance, in the example of the friend who comes to settle the difference between a husband and wife, the "counteraction" may be the fact of the friend's love for the young woman. Striving honestly to help the marriage, he must hide the fact of his love. There may be other obstacles, such as the husband, who might not want to listen to his well-meaning friend. Overcoming such obstacles keeps an actor from becoming careless and makes him carry out his action more vividly, with more energy and strength.

Each character in a play always has his own main object of struggle.

The Super-Objective and the Through Line of Actions

Stanislavski stated over and over that without great playwrights there would not be theater, that the first duty of the theater is toward the playwright, and is to project his idea dynamically. A written play is transformed into a performance by the actors and the director, who must transmit to the public the author's main idea, his reason for having written the play. To carry across the main idea, or the *super-objective*, as Stanislavski called it, is the final goal of every performance and is the point of departure for the Stanislavski System.

The super-objective, which is the essence of the play, must guide the director and the interpretation of characters and events. With the super-objective an actor weaves the idea of the author into the theatrical performance. The super-objective is the basic stimulus of a creative process; the theatrical form and the

written play should unite through a continual fertil-
ization of each other in the process of building a
performance.

The super-objective controls each character's logic
of actions, which makes the theme concrete. While an
actor is preparing his role the super-objective must be
clear in his mind from the beginning through its very
end. To forget it, as Stanislavski said, is to break the
line of life portrayed on stage. Every detail, every
thought, every action, must be closely related to it.

An actor should give a proper and expressive name
to the super-objective, which should be an active verb.
The interpretation of the play depends on it.

For an actor's performance to have logical order and
perspective, he should mentally trace a line which will
run through his role. Stanislavski called this the
through line of actions. This is the active execution of
the super-objective, the profound organic tie uniting
the independent parts of the role. The through line of
action leads an actor to the main purpose of his
activities and prevents him from being distracted by
secondary events; it is the consecutive incarnation of
the super-objective in scenic actions. It is the under-
current of the play, the inner content of events
expressed in action. The super-objective and the
through line of actions are the aims to which the
building of a role is subordinate. Every element of the
Stanislavski System is subordinate to them.

An actor must continually check his through line of
action to make sure that he has the right activity,
order, logic, color, contrast, and that all these elements
contribute to the projection of the super-objective.

Determination of actions must be guided by the through line of actions. To be consecutive and logical, each action must depend on the previous one and on the following one. The through line of actions is all the character's actions interwoven logically, having the same purpose of expressing the main idea.

Every character has some basic, main purpose in the circumstances given by the playwright. Such a purpose could be called central action, and reflects the character's most important strivings. This aim through the role is the character's own super-objective and his through line of action. It is the movement of the inner world of the character. The aim toward which a character is striving in an act, a scene, or an episode, is called the *main action* of these sections. To interpret his role, an actor must find its super-objective. Conflict in a play is developed by the through line of actions and the counteraction of the characters.

The search for the super-objective, for the through line of action, and for the theme of a role was called by Stanislavski "the reconnaissance of the mind."

Just as he has a super-objective and the through line of actions in a role, an actor must have them in every exercise or improvisation.

The Actor's
Physical Apparatus

An actor must make sure that in creating a character he does not lose a single nuance, or any physical or psychological means which would help to express his inner experience. A slight movement of the head, a change in the direction of a look, can tell something about the inner life of the character and project his thoughts.

The quality of an actor's performance depends not only upon the creation of the inner life of a role but also upon the physical embodiment of it. Stanislavski said that imperfection in the external expression of a role can disfigure a profound conception of the playwright. In order to embody the subtle inner life of a character, an actor must have at his command responsive and sensitive physical means. An actor's own organism is his instrument. Actions are his material. In order to build favorable conditions for creativeness, the instrument of the actor's organism must be prepared. Bad enunciation indicates a lack of elementary respect for the audience. It is tiresome for the spectator to listen to an actor whose speech is not precise and comprehensible. Defects in speech, of course, will distort a performance. To "paint a picture" with vivid colors, an actor must use the whole scale of his voice. An actor's voice must be trained like that of a singer and be placed in the "masque," the front of the face, where there are resonators. Speech on stage is as important an art as singing for a singer. When an actor has well-developed respiration, good clear diction, and a trained voice, he will not have to force, but instead will be able to speak naturally and softly, and even his whisper will be heard everywhere in the theater.

Muscular tension, the reaction to an audience, interferes with the actor's execution of natural physical actions and therefore with the correct inner state and the inner experience. To cope with muscular tension an actor needs a trained responsive body and control over his muscles. Even the slightest tension of muscles can paralyze an actor's creative state. Through systematic work, an actor will develop an "observer" inside himself, who will watch and instantly find the spot of unnecessary tension and as instantly eliminate it. This will become a natural, automatic habit. Concentration on a specific thought and a concrete action helps the actor to relax.

Stanislavski believed in training the body to improve posture and to make movements supple, graceful, and finished. An actor must, however, bear in mind that there is no place in the living theater for mannerisms or mechanical gestures. An actor should not use a gesture because it is graceful or plastic. A gesture must reflect an inner experience. It will then become a purposeful, logical, and truthful movement.

"As a creative, artistic force, you do not differ from pianists and singers, and must practice every day," Stanislavski said to his actors. The actor's body and voice must be cultivated and trained to be able to express externally, instantly and precisely, the delicate inner experiences of the creative process. The inner and physical apparatus of an actor must be trained simultaneously. While the inner technique cultivates an actor's ability to evoke the proper state without which creativity is impossible, and which depends on an action executed with the help of all the elements of Stanislavski's inner technique, the physical technique will make an actor's physical apparatus capable of expressing inner processes and of embodying the spiritual life of the character. "With an untrained body it is impossible to transmit the subconscious creativeness, just as it is impossible to play the Ninth Symphony by Beethoven on instruments out of tune," said Stanislavski.

The physical technique will train an actor's feeling for truth and form. Stanislavski attributed a vital role to technical mastery. He demanded that actors work on rhythm, gesture, acrobatics, enunciation, voice, expressive speech, and historical ceremonies. He considered it elementary and obligatory for an actor to control his voice and body, to move well, to know how to wear a costume.

An actor who searches not only for inner content but also for external form will understand the significance of every detail which has to do with the new being on the stage. The right costume for the role becomes part of it. The moment of putting on the costume has great psychological significance for an actor. He must learn to wear it, and to use a sword, a fan, a cape, or a shawl.

An actor's performance must have a clear and precise pattern of speech and movement. Every form of expression must be simple and clear. Every movement, gesture, intonation must be precise, expressive, finished from an artistic point of view. Only the mastery of physical technique will assure the necessary freedom to permit an actor to execute a natural, truthful physical action and give himself to the experiences of the character. Few know or remember that Stanislavski said that the art of the theater is based on the union of the deep substance of the inner life and a beautiful, light, expressive form of it. The expressiveness of the art, the entire performance, depends on this union. Theater art is subject to the same law that governs all the arts: the union of profound content and artistic form.

Work on the Role:
Building a Character

There are no small roles—only small actors.
MOTTO OF THE MOSCOW ART THEATER

Love the art in yourself, not yourself in the art.
STANISLAVSKI

Every art has its own means of expression. Poets have words, musicians have sounds, painters have colors. An actor's means of expression is the human action, which, as we have seen, is a psychophysical process. Spectators learn about the characters on stage the way we learn about people in life—through their physical actions, which are dictated by their aims. An action explains what a character does at a given moment and why he does it. Every aim (psychological) is expressed physically, and conversely every physical movement has its aim. Movements disclose a person's interests, tastes, habits, moods. The complex of human psychological life is expressed through a simple physical action. The logic of a person's physical actions gives us an understanding of his inner experiences. Without the union of the psychological and the physical a role cannot be built. Life will be created on the stage if an actor follows the laws of nature.

It is important for an actor to see the character he builds in terms of actions. In two and a half hours on the stage, an actor must project "the life of a human spirit"; during every moment, therefore, he must use actions which will express that life. The creative process of an actor's work is choice of actions, and the whole Stanislavski System is called upon to help that process. If an action helps to express the character, it is artistically right; if it does not, it is wrong. An action cannot be accidental or superfluous. The choice of actions must be guided by the *main idea* of the play and of the role.

The choice of actions, then, is the foundation on which a character is built. Executing certain actions, the actor builds one character; executing others, he builds another character. The value of an action lies in the inner content that it expresses. An actor becomes an actor when he masters the process of choosing actions to build a definite character, said Stanislavski.

An action on stage, if it has no purpose, merely diverts the audience's attention from the essence of the play. The purpose is what determines the action, and that purpose is to express individual life. In order that an action should be truthful, an actor must be able to answer several questions: "Who am I?" "Where is the action taking place?" "With whom?" "What for?" He must know all the details of the given circumstances. The role is ready when an actor knows concretely *what* the character does each moment on the stage and *why* he does it. The actions concretize the life of a human spirit, and give the audience an idea of the character's habits, moods, tastes.

An actor must create an individual logic of actions, unique for each character. In every action there is something objective, common to all, but at the same time each person's logic of action is individual and right only for him. For instance, if we want fresh air, we may open a window. But, because the background and the interests of people differ, different people will open a window in different ways. Each movement of a person's inner life, each reaction to what happens around him, is unique. The correct definition of actions for each character will be determined not by the intuition of an actor but by his deep analysis of the intention of the author and by his own ability to choose that which is most characteristic and typical in the character. As we have seen, Stanislavski attributed enormous importance to the verbal determination of actions, because such definition forces an actor to think and to study the role and the whole play. "The art of an actor," said Stanislavski, "is the knowledge of the logic of actions in a play and the ability to put them all on one thread in a consecutive order." All the actions must lead to the fulfillment of the main idea of the play and the role.

The continuous line of the character's actions, leading to the solution of the super-objective, builds *perspective* in a role. Attention to such perspective is obligatory in scenic work because it will help the harmonious relationship and distribution of everything an actor does in his role. (An actor must clearly divide the perspective in the life of his character from that of his own.) When an actor has perspective he adds variety, contrast, coloring, and shading to his role's various moments. He distributes all the elements of his role in a harmonious way in the interests of the play, and his role grows logically.

The behavior of a character must be composed of small, logical, concrete actions. Every action must be consecutive, as in life, in life's tempo-rhythm, and must have as much concentration as it requires in real life. Spectators are interested only in concrete actions; the greatest impression on them is made by a simple, correctly, and truthfully executed physical action. The importance that Stanislavski attached to an actor's ability to fulfill the action cannot be overemphasized. The actions lead him into the inner world of the character. To perform an action truthfully means to live on stage.

Stanislavski called a *word* the physical side of the psychophysical action. Images in our mind and the "subtext"—the meaning behind the words which make us say them—are the psychological side of the action. According to Stanislavski, the subtext is the inward "life of a human spirit" that constantly flows under the words of a role. It has the same function in speech that the through line of action has in the field of action. Words are only a part of a given moment on stage and are born of thoughts, images, and bodily expressions of these inner processes.

It is important to understand the attitudes of the character. In life our intonations disclose our attitudes; to act through words, an actor must speak "to the eye," not to the ear, of his fellow actor. He must see images and transmit them to his partner. He must prepare this at home, and check it during a rehearsal. If he ignores these images, an actor makes the same mistake as when he uses movements only. If he transmits images and fulfills his actions, he is active and his emotions are stirred. Images must grow in detail and become richer. If an actor wants the words to be his own, he must understand the reason for which the author gave them to the character. A character's lines will be alive if he needs them—i.e., if he has a purpose in saying them and makes others see his purpose. If he strives honestly and energetically to fulfill his actions, his words are "active" and the audience understands what he wants to say. Intonations will become colorful through the images in an actor's mind, through his enunciation, through his projecting the objective, through the use of the active word. Mechanical memorizing kills the imagination.

"A word with a crumpled beginning is like a man with a squashed head," said Stanislavski. "A word without an end reminds me of a man with amputated legs. Careless pronunciation of sounds and syllables is the same as having a broken tooth, a damaged eye, or a cut ear."

"Treasure the spoken word," said Stanislavski. The energetic word is the most powerful means of stirring emotions, the most expressive and most valuable of physical actions in the process of building a character. The word is the result of thoughts, feelings, and images expressed by the body. For an actor the word is a *verbal action*, which means that when he speaks he is in a process of action through words. Verbal action is determined by its purpose. The word influences another person's intellect, imagination, and emotions. An actor must know which of these three he wants to influence in another actor. His own speech will have to be logical and convincing. He will have to analyze the text of each event in his role, know his action (for instance, to convince, to console, to reproach); he must know which thought is the most important, and with which arguments he can prove it, which word in each phrase is the most important for expression of the thought, and so on. If an actor knows what he wants from his partner, his words will become verbal actions and will involve his emotions. "To speak means to act," said Stanislavski. And when we listen to others we first hear and then see images of what we have heard, and then our body expresses these inner processes. Trying to influence his fellow actor with his words, an actor makes known the character he portrays. If the audience does not understand what an actor is saying, the fault lies not alone in defective enunciation. The verbal action depends on the physical action.

Stanislavski demanded that actors thoroughly study the play and the author's mentality. An actor must understand the main idea of the play; he must see himself as a part of the whole. Work on the role means study of the spiritual content of the play and understanding of the "kernel" from which it came to birth. It is this kernel that determines the essence of the play. Only after understanding the main idea of the author will the actors and the director begin to feel and to see the characters of future performances. The main idea is the spine and pulse of the play, of which the character is a single element; the actor must know his mission in the chain of events of the play, his responsibility to make the main idea live. In the theme of his role, which he must see clearly, every detail, every thought and gesture must be imbued with the light of the main idea of the play. He should not make hasty decisions about the character.

The few moments seen on stage are closely connected with the whole life of the character and even with his future. An actor must go through much the same creative process the playwright went through. He must complete the life of his character in his imagination and see a continuous, logical, unbroken chain of events. Nemirovich-Danchenko called this whole life of the character, which is unseen but must be sensed on the stage, the "second plan." All the experiences that have influenced the character throughout his life will help an actor build his role with justification. Stanislavski believed what great dramatists believe: that if you treat the character as a live human being, he functions naturally and in a way that even the author might not expect.

A character, according to Stanislavski, is the flesh and the soul of the actor and is born of the union of all spiritual and physical elements of the role and the actor. Only such a new being can exist, can *be*. In building a character, an actor should be influenced by the playwright, by the director, by contact with the other performers, and by all the hints about the character that are found in the script. A character is a human being with his own thoughts, actions, appearance, mannerisms, experiences, habits, and so on.

Though conceived by the author, the character must express the actor's individual ideas, his emotions, his intuitions—analogous, of course, to those of the character. Only when the actor's personality fuses with that of the character will he live the role. Facing a new personality in every new play, an actor has the possibility of endless discovery. It is the inner world that must attract the attention of the audience.

If an actor wants to impress the audience with the "truth of passions," as Pushkin called it, he must follow the Stanislavski formula, "Go from yourself." An actor cannot and should not reject his own *"I,"* if the character is to be alive. He must become another person while remaining himself, using his own organic nature, his personality, as material in the creation of a character. But "Go from yourself" does not mean playing oneself, as dilettantes think. It does not mean going on stage without having analyzed and chosen the character's thoughts, actions, and feelings. "It is a disaster if every role, every playwright, is adapted to oneself. It means death to the art," said Stanislavski. "There are actors and especially actresses who are not interested in characterization or 'reincarnation' because they adjust every role to themselves and depend only on their own charm. On this they build their success. Without it they are as helpless as Samson without his hair. We know many cases where an actor's personal charm was the cause of his ruin because his only preoccupation was to demonstrate himself. Naturalness for the sake of naturalness is worse than robbery. An actor must adjust himself to the role, not the role to himself." With his "Go from yourself," Stanislavski meant that in building the logic of a character's actions the actor must first search for what is general, shared with his own logic of actions. An actor who tries to be always naïvely natural and cute does not contribute to the art of the theater. To be natural himself is not the same as being natural as the character. Actors must learn the goal of their art: *reincarnation*. They must learn to build a variety of unusual characters and to discover their essence but to remain themselves, true and sincere on the stage.

There is nothing mystical, no mysterious transformation, in the Stanislavski reincarnation. An actor achieves reincarnation when he achieves the truthful behavior of the character, when his actions are interwoven with words and thoughts, when he has searched for all the necessary traits of a given character, when he surrounds himself with its given circumstances and becomes so accustomed to them that he does not know where his own personality leaves off and that of the character begins. Stanislavski considered reincarnation the height of the actor's art. Creating the character is the essence of the theater, for it is through characters that a dramatist unfolds the theme for his play.

Although intuition plays an important part in it, the building of a character—with its variety of thoughts, actions, and feelings—cannot be mastered through that faculty alone. In the process of building a character, an actor must collect all the possible details and characteristic traits. Sometimes he can find them in the reserve of his memories and impress them on the concrete character. But he should learn to take them from the infinite source which is life around him. He must know how to choose typical material for different characters and use it. Stanislavski insisted that an actor should learn to take material for his creations from the life around him, from people he knows, or even from those he sees in the street and who leave an impression on him. In life's continual change, in its innumerable faces, types, costumes, and so on, such source for material is unlimited. "Take examples from life and nature," said Mikhail Shchepkin. "A vivid feeling of reality and the ability to express it creates the poet," said Goethe. "Genius," said Stanislavski, "is an actor who sees life and is able to re-create it on the stage."

An actor must gradually discard the superfluous, because only what is necessary lives on the stage. An actor should use only the details that help to individualize a particular personality. A single characteristic external detail can emphasize a thought and sometimes be more expressive than a whole monologue.

A role must be connected with everyone and everything around it. An actor must establish relationships with other characters. He must know how he feels about everything in the play and must have active, sharp reactions to everybody and to everything. He must know the environment he is to reflect with his portrayal. He must study the behavior of the character. Whatever an actor does in his role, his clothes, his speech, and his movements must be characteristic of the person he portrays.

The Stanislavski rule, "When you play a nasty man, search for what is good in him," contributes to the creation of different facets of a character and thus makes the man's nastiness appear sharper. Trying to project only evil makes the performance heavy and dull.

Between two sentences in a dialogue there is an *inner monologue*—a direct connection which is hidden. Before an actor can answer his fellow actor, he must evaluate in his thoughts the other's behavior. His body must express the evaluation in his mind. The lines, thoughts, and actions of the partner are material for thinking over the answer. When an actor reflects, evaluates, controls his own desires, tries to understand, analyzes, and judges, he executes an inner action. In real life one takes a decision before executing a certain external action. Thoughts must be significant to deserve an actor's concentration. Today's actor must be capable of thinking as the character would, seriously and deeply. Unfortunately, actors often believe that to listen is just to look at the fellow actor and not to think at all. Many actors rest while others are speaking lines and come to life only when they have to speak their own. In order that his character may live a continuous life on stage, an actor must have inner monologues, expressed by his body, when another character speaks, for he must react inwardly and outwardly to everything that takes place on stage. There are silences and pauses on stage; these, too, an actor must fill with active thoughts to make the life on stage continuous.

A *monologue*—thinking aloud—expresses the thoughts, feelings, and mood of the character. In a monologue, an actor must complete the text with the inner thoughts required by pauses.

Stanislavski said that because life is a continuous struggle, on stage as in life there are counteractions of other persons, facts, circumstances, events, opposing a logic of actions. Conflicts and struggles create interesting collisions. A valuable dramatic work is always based on struggles between different persons. Spectators are carried away by the process of a struggle. A person is pushed to act, to express his own interests, when these interests clash with the environment. An actor must find the obstacles in the way of his character and try to overcome them. For instance, if he has a secret to tell another person and he thinks that people may hear him, or that somebody may come in and he will not have time to tell it, such imaginary but logical obstacles will force him to fulfill his objective more vividly. Each character has its own main object of struggle.

Musical comedy, which requires great skill, needs actors who sing well, dance well, speak well, and can build a character in the same way as dramatic actors. The lighter the style of the show, the quicker should be the changes in the character's inner experience, and therefore they should be more intense. Transitions from words to singing and dancing are difficult and must be mastered. Actors in musical comedy, besides being musical, rhythmical, and knowing how to move lightly and to control their bodies, must be able to justify each event, even the most improbable situation, and know how to change easily from one state to another. There is no difference between the truth of existence in dramatic scenes and in dancing or vocal scenes. An actor must behave as if it were indispensable to sing or to dance through the logic of his character. Vocal and dance training should include definite actions. In a chorus, as in crowd scenes in a dramatic play, each performer must determine his behavior and know his attitude toward other characters and the events in the play.

Many great men of the theater have thought that a movement of the actor's highly trained body would stir his emotions. Meyerhold's "biomechanics," with the help of which he expected to achieve the actor's emotional involvement, eventually disappointed him, although it remains a valid physical exercise and is used as such today in Russian drama schools. Another system, "expressive movement," promulgated by Delsarte, as we have seen, has been superseded by the Stanislavski System.

A *poem* must be recited so that its musical and rhythmic beauties are revealed. An actor must know to whom he is speaking it and what his objective is in saying it. Just as when he works on a role, he must know the "second plan," have a continuous film of images, an inner monologue, and an expressive body which will justify his saying the poem in the elevated mood that it requires.

An actor must continually control his behavior on stage. He must learn to see the behavior of the character he portrays and correct it if necessary. The method of physical actions gives an actor an exceptional opportunity to unite the functioning subconscious with conscious control.

An actor's conscious watching of the character's behavior does not harm the quality of the performance. Stanislavski emphatically demanded that an actor have uninterrupted, conscious control of his behavior on stage. Reactions of the audience can help an actor to be aware of the result of his work and sometimes to correct his faults on the spot. "The audience is a huge mirror reflecting the actor's creativity," said Stanislavski. "We must learn to look into this mirror and see what we create. An actor must act as the character and listen as an actor." And the famous Italian tragic actor Tommaso Salvini (1829–1916) said, "An actor lives, cries, and laughs on stage, but he never stops watching his tears and his laughter." An actor without self-control is not acceptable on stage.

It is especially important to point out this demand for conscious control because of a tendency among actors to consider their creativity as the expression of "subconscious" and "unconscious" strivings. The Stanislavski System never permits an actor to be in the power of a blind and accidental intuition. The System is indeed conscious activity at its height, preparing a favorable ground for inspiration, or for subconscious creativity, when the actor's whole psychophysical apparatus is involved. Such subconscious activity is the goal of an actor's art, and is achieved by the actor who has mastered his technique. Stanislavski's demands for conscious activity kept increasing.

Stanislavski did not believe in ready-made results for an actor's creativeness. He demanded that the actor create anew at each performance the live organic process after carefully studying and developing the character's logic of actions. An actor should not repeat yesterday's performance: he should create each day a new, true life as if it were happening on stage for the first time. The Stanislavski formula "Today, here, now" makes every performance different, when every gesture, intonation, and facial expression will be fresh.

Some actors insist on using their small, charming clichés. An actor is often tempted by what he has already found to be successful; he thinks this makes his work easier. New, even brilliant discoveries for one role may become clichés that hurt another role. It requires courage to experiment and to reject what has already been found successful; only if an actor fights repetition will he be able to bring out each time his real creative individuality. While working on a character, an actor must forget all the roles he has created previously, and must build a completely new one each time.

In preparing his role, besides improvisations on his actions an actor should play improvisations on various situations in which the character might find himself but which are not in the play. Lines that are not given by the author, but which the character might say, should be spoken in improvisations. Thoughts, actions, and images must be prepared by the actor at home, where he should say the text in his mind only, not aloud. He must see in his mind his partner and what he says.

Physical characterization, which must express the inner life, will come gradually as an actor works on his role. External characteristics are the result of deep penetration into the character's inner world. An actor should learn to sit, to walk, to dress as an old man, as a fat or a weak one, and so on. At home he should practice his everyday activities as the character—dressing, eating, washing, reading, as the character would.

An actor's mastership, his ability to perform in various kinds of plays—for instance, the tragedies of Shakespeare or Schiller—will depend on the union of his inner and external techniques.

There is danger in an actor's trying to set a definite form for his role too early. He must bear in mind that at no time has he reached the limits. "Art is search, not final form," said Vakhtangov. If what an actor finds is good, it will be easy to find something better. Even after the opening of the play the role should grow.

Stanislavski demanded a creative attitude toward each performance. An actor should arrive at the theater well ahead of his entrance. Besides putting on his costume and make-up, he must go over the important points of his role. He must make inner readjustments, "the *toilette*" of an actor, as Stanislavski called it.

Looking at the stage and orienting himself will put the actor into the proper relationship to the objects on the stage; seeing why they are there will make him feel comfortable. An actor must know the whole day's activity of his character and what might have happened to him before he appears. The actor should start playing a minute or two before he goes on, and move gradually and logically to the moment of his entrance. He should think only of one action at a time.

P. M. Ershov, in his *Directing As Practical Psychology*, writes, "No matter how important sincerity is in art, it is not sufficient. Every sleeping man is absolutely sincere, as is every person who experiences physical pain. . . . For art, there must be expressive form."

The Director

The director must die within an actor.

VLADIMIR I. NEMIROVICH-DANCHENKO

The director is the organizer of a performance, the interpreter of a play. He creates new values by transposing a play from its literary form into its theatrical form. The director must know life; he must be a psychologist with an artist's sensitivity. He must be able to evaluate and analyze the play; to express the main idea of the author; to explain the play to the actors and stir their interest; to suggest ways of realizing specific problems; to make use of the conflicts in the script; to demonstrate if necessary; to find the right rhythm; to give brief, concrete instructions; and to foresee the audience's reactions.

The director must have imagination and be capable of invention; he must have culture, taste, tact—and principles. A director sometimes tries too hard to establish his own prestige. He has no right to distort the idea of the author for the sake of his own inventions, but he has a right to insist on the realization of his ideas.

82

A director who knows acting technique is likely to be more patient than others, because he knows what is easy and what is difficult for an actor. Work with actors is the important part of the director's task of creating a performance; his guidance should help the actor even in future work in other plays.

The director must sense an actor's individuality and be able to create the whole with various individualities. This, however, does not mean that he should adapt himself to an actor. The director should not demand the same colors from different actors. Neither should he demand definite results, a definite expression or gesture or intonation, at the very start. Rehearsals will proceed well after the director's idea has reached the actors. This will be achieved through discussion, when the director checks his ideas with the group. All the parts of the production should be discussed one by one. Actors must be given the opportunity to talk about the play—its main idea, its events, its through line of action, and the relationships among its characters. However, I heard Stanislavski impress on actors that rehearsals exist for work, for action, and for search —not for protracted discussions, as some followers of the System insist on today. If an actor has mastered the technique and is able to analyze a play through consecutive actions in the given circumstances of the author, he will not wander in his independent work, and will not waste time in meaningless discussion.

Even a director with the most unconventional ideas must make sure that his actors live the characters' experiences through the laws developed by Stanislavski. In early rehearsals only the truth of an actor's behavior should be watched. Organic truth is vital, but the director must see that everything has a vivid form and that the truth is interesting and expressive. A director must see the play in terms of actions and should speak of them, not of feelings; he should suggest at once that actors analyze actions even while reading the play the first time, in order to avoid monotonous intonations.

Blocking out the play forces the actor to analyze the actions; the director should be able to help the actor to determine them and try them out. Improvised lines will help him to understand the necessity and efficiency of a certain action. The method of analysis through events and actions must be applied throughout the play. Using his own words, the actor will be forced to search for the precise action and may find unexpected adaptations. The director must lead actors to logical, purposeful actions leading to the superobjective of the play and help them to understand all the nuances in their partners' behavior.

The director may have a preliminary pattern for his production, but staging is a creative process, and he must be able to improvise. Each *mise en scène* will be expressive when—even without words—it projects the content, the situation.

Before actors and the director work on the lines, they must go through a process similar to that of the playwright, completing the life of each character in order to understand the thoughts and feelings that dictate the characters' words.

If an actor is incapable of executing a direction, the director must make sure that he himself is not at fault.

He might have given the actor the wrong task, and suggested an inappropriate attitude toward an event. The actor's problem may be a lack of justification for a specific action, and it is the director who must see that every action is justified. The actor's difficulty may be a lack of creative "nourishment," and talks with the director about the life to be portrayed may be helpful. An actor's trying to act an emotion, or even a little falsehood in some detail, could be another problem.

The director must see that the idea of the entire play, as well as every thought in each scene and in each phrase of the author's text, is brought to maximum concreteness and clarity. As Meyerhold said, "The director must toss thoughts into the audience." He must see to it that all the elements—such as sets, music, lights, and costumes—contribute to the whole performance; every pose, every *mise en scène* must bring out the inner content of the given moment on the stage. He must be able to "hear" each performer, each element of the performance as though it were an instrument in an orchestra.

The form of the production will be found when the director has his super-super-objective—his need to contribute to society—has his artistic views, and knows *what* he wants to say and *why* he wants to say it. When the director knows the answers, the form he finds will express the inner content of the play. The director's solution is senseless if he does not understand what he wants to say and why. He must find the unique form for each play.

"Directing," said Stanislavski, "is a precise science, not vague thoughts and fantasy."

Eugene Vakhtangov:
the Disciple

Stanislavski's greatest pupil, Eugene Bogrationovich Vakhtangov, was born on February 1, 1883, in Vladikavkaz (now Dzaudzhikau), North Caucasus region, Russia. After being graduated from *gimnasia* (high school) he went to Moscow to study in the university. The Moscow Art Theater made a great impression on him, and he began to be active in several dramatic groups. The fact that he wished to become an actor shocked his father, who had expected his son to follow him in the prosperous tobacco business; the two quarreled and never became reconciled.

During the eight years between *gimnasia* and his acceptance into the Moscow Art Theater in 1911, Vakhtangov played about fifty roles and staged about twenty plays. In 1909, he had entered a drama school directed by A. I. Adashev, an actor of the Moscow Art Theater, and had met Leopold Antonovich Sulerzhitski, who taught there. Neither an actor nor a professional director, Sulerzhitski was an enthusiast of the theater, believing it to be a powerful cultural, moral, and aesthetic influence. Actors, he believed, should be educated for such an important profession. Stanislavski considered Sulerzhitski a genius and was under his influence, as Vakhtangov was soon to be. Sulerzhitski played an important role in helping Stanislavski by using his experimental techniques with students in the Adashev school. Thus Vakhtangov learned about the System at the very beginning, and at once became Sulerzhitski's favorite. He was impressed by Stanislavski and by Sulerzhitski's views on the influence that a performance can have on an audience.

In the autumn of 1911, when Vakhtangov was accepted at the Moscow Art Theater, he was in direct contact with Stanislavski and with Nemirovich-Danchenko, the great director and co-founder of the Moscow Art Theater. Vakhtangov dedicated himself to fighting all "theatricality," which, at that time, he considered the principal source of bad acting. He believed completely in Stanislavski's teachings about building true life on the stage, and was convinced that the essence of theater was the building of "the life of the human spirit." He was deeply impressed by Stanislavski's way of analyzing a play to discover its essence. He became the System's strongest adherent and soon became Stanislavski's assistant.

Stanislavski was categorically against any final formulation or publication of his experimental work. Between 1912 and 1917, when his System was coming into existence, Vakhtangov, too, was searching for subtle means of discovering the inner life of a character, and he felt equally strongly about those who wrote on theories of Stanislavski which had not yet been published. As Stanislavski anticipated, his teachings were often distorted.

Stanislavski's goal became Vakhtangov's: to discover the idea of the play through the play's characters. To do this, Vakhtangov believed actors must learn "reincarnation" by creating and living the inner experiences of the characters. As no one else had, Vakhtangov quickly grasped the importance of Stanislavski's teachings, and Stanislavski recognized Vakhtangov's immense talent and his faith in his System. He was soon giving Vakhtangov one assignment after another; he asked him to make a list of exercises, to work on scenes, and to show them to him; he was pleased with the results. The old actors of the Moscow Art Theater, who had resented the System, were deeply impressed and began to study it themselves.

Vakhtangov was soon in great demand among the numerous Moscow theatrical groups. Drama schools competed for his time. In poor health but full of enthusiasm, Vakhtangov taught what he had learned from Stanislavski. Vakhtangov was the first to teach young actors that their task is not only to find the right intonation and to "feel" the role, but to learn the science of acting. "An actor must live and think as the character," he said. "The character is the organic union of the life of the character and the life of the actor. An actor must assimilate the character's life." Vakhtangov taught his students to observe in such a way as not only to copy the external line of behavior but to understand the unbreakable tie between the inner life of a person and its external expression. He taught them to bring on stage the unexpected, interesting truth, not the worn-out one. An actor, he said, must offer something new to those who come to see him. And, like Stanislavski, he believed that in the theater everyone is equally important—every actor, every stagehand. His actors also learned what it meant to be in love with art. To teach the System, as Vakhtangov himself said, was the mission of his life.

On January 15, 1913, a group of young actors whom Stanislavski had entrusted to Vakhtangov became the First Studio of the Moscow Art Theater under the guidance of Stanislavski and Sulerzhitski. In November of the same year, Vakhtangov staged a play by Hauptmann called *Festival of Peace* in the First Studio. He succeeded in making the actors live the characters' inner experiences, but Stanislavski was highly critical of his failure to restrain them from what he called "inner hysteria." This, said Stanislavski, was acting "in a trance," which he considered a deformity. The actors were performing for themselves, he said, not for the audience.

That same year, a group of young people came to Vakhtangov and told him that although they did not want to become professional actors they were eager to learn what the theater could offer them. Vakhtangov agreed to teach them. To help the group financially, Vakhtangov, in 1914, agreed to stage *Lanin's Estate* by Boris Zaitsev. He did not like the play but had yielded to his students' enthusiasm for it. The production was such a complete failure that Stanislavski and Nemiro-

vich-Danchenko forbade Vakhtangov to work outside
the Moscow Art Theater and the First Studio. However, Vakhtangov continued to work with this group°
secretly; it soon became the Vakhtangov Studio and
later was called the Third Studio of the Moscow Art
Theater; after Vakhtangov's death it became the
Vakhtangov Theater. There he had the artistic freedom for which he had longed.

In 1914, Vakhtangov created his best role,
Tackleton in the First Studio's dramatization of Dick-
ens' *Cricket on the Hearth*. Without losing the organic
truth of the role, he had become the master of sharp
expressiveness; clearly and precisely he disclosed the
inner essence of the character through the external
form. In 1915, Vakhtangov staged his second work at
the First Studio, a play by H. Berger called *The
Deluge*. Both directorial works were in the tradition of
the Moscow Art Theater. At this point Vakhtangov
leaned more to naturalism than Stanislavski ever did.
When Stanislavski made some changes in *The Deluge*,
Vakhtangov accused him of being too theatrical and of
working against his own principles. However, there
were some embryonic hints of what he was to express
in later works.

In staging Ibsen's *Rosmersholm* in 1918, Vakhtangov
demanded complete "reincarnation" without the help
of costumes, sets, or make-up. He insisted that the
actors must believe what the characters believe. This
was still the early Vakhtangov, who believed that
actors must develop in themselves the characters'

° This group was called the Mansurovskaya Studio.

points of view. Any difference between the actor and the character must be erased, he said, and an actor must think not *about* the character but only *as* the character. Some critics accused Vakhtangov of being too much under the influence of Expressionism, which was then fashionable, especially in Germany. The Vakhtangov of 1911–1918 was carrying Stanislavski's ideas to an extreme.

From one extreme, Vakhtangov went to another, and took as his motto: "Play your point of view of the character, not the character." But Stanislavski, who had begun to review his own ideas about the actor's identification with the character, stated that to merge with the character does not mean that an actor must entirely approve of him. The character's mentality, intentions, and feelings must be evaluated, he said, but an actor need not have the same mentality. An actor must understand the essence of the character, but, if necessary, he must be critical about it. The essence of the character must be disclosed through the logic of actions. It is possible for the actor to become the character and at the same time to disapprove of him or accuse him, said Stanislavski.

Soon afterward, Vakhtangov began to proclaim, that "In theater there must be *theater*." *He gave a different kind of importance to the actor's use of his personal experiences*. There are better ways to build a live character, he said. He made it clear that an actor's own emotions are worthless unless they reach the audience, that there is no art if an actor's tears do not affect the audience. Following Stanislavski's teachings, Vakhtangov searched for the strongest means to affect the actor, who, in turn, would affect the audience. He refused to allow accidental behavior on stage—accidental details which did not express anything. An intuitive, logical solution is the result of logical, conscious work. The subconscious, he said, would function if it received nourishment sent to it by the actor consciously. Stanislavski was then in the process of searching for a "conscious means to the subconscious."

Since Vakhtangov's own childhood had been unhappy, he had at first planned to give much attention to his son. But his wife and child seldom saw him. Vakhtangov rehearsed during the day, performed at night, and worked with the actors on the System after a performance. His reputation grew; he remained dedicated to the realization of Stanislavski's goals. He dreamed of a studio as the heart of the theater. And he dreamed of a school to provide new talent continually. He aimed to educate actors and directors. He longed to find epic plays which would represent the spirit of the times.

In 1920, Vakhtangov staged Chekhov's *The Wedding* in his Studio. At first he demanded from actors only the truth in the play's circumstances. But when he restaged it in 1921, he led the performers to extremes of external characterization. Magnified characters that grew into symbols now became characteristic of all Vakhtangov's productions. In *The Wedding*, he satirized the world of the *petit-bourgeois* and projected Chekhov's condemnation of such life.

But it was with his new version of Maeterlinck's *The*

Miracle of Saint Anthony,° with which the Third Studio opened its new theater in November 1921, that Vakhtangov marked his establishment of theatrical form. Greatly exaggerated externally, it was always alive within. The precision and rhythm of the performance were on the highest artistic level. The paradox was striking; the comedy was now a tragic farce. The only live human beings, the saint and the maiden, moved among dead figures, whose automatic movements instantly stopped in strange formations. Vakhtangov made actors into character-symbols through sharp satire of the mannerisms of the Belgian bourgeoisie. He did not permit the uncontrolled expression of inner life; every movement, gesture, intonation had to be studied thoroughly. Actors were made to achieve clear, precise form. Every idea, he said, demands its own form of expression, and the idea and the form of each work are unique, unrepeatable. Vakhtangov did not decide the form in advance; it developed through the discovery of the essence of the play. *The Miracle of Saint Anthony* aroused enormous interest. Vakhtangov was now considered the progressive director who would lead the theater to new heights.

Vakhtangov staged Strindberg's *Erik XIV* at the First Studio. In working on it he emphasized that he was following Stanislavski's principles of inner technique merged with external form. It was Stanislavski who emphasized the importance of word, phrase, voice, thought, gesture, rhythm, plastic movement, he said; the First Studio was searching for expressive

° Vakhtangov had staged the first version in 1918.

theatrical form for true inner experiences. *Erik XIV*
opened in 1921 and was met with both admiration and
criticism; it provoked heated discussions.

The form of *Erik XIV* was so different from what
had been done before that it was considered a
revolution in the Moscow Art Theater and the First
Studio. Vakhtangov projected his interpretation of the
play through every gesture, pose, and scene. Costumes
were stylized, and the make-up created an impression
of masks of suffering. Stanislavski approved of it; the
form was thoroughly justified and the actors lived on
stage. Vakhtangov had clearly achieved new heights in
the theater.

While Vakhtangov worked on *Erik XIV*, Stanislavski
was staging Gogol's *The Inspector-General*. The brilliant actor Michael Chekhov rehearsed the leading
roles in both plays. Vakhtangov helped Chekhov to
achieve Stanislavski's demands, and the results ob-
tained by Chekhov under the two directors were
remarkable. Michael Chekhov's Khlestakov in the
Gogol play was overwhelming in its grotesqueness.
Vakhtangov was jubilant; he saw that Stanislavski also
was trying to go beyond naturalism. Stanislavski was so
impressed by what Vakhtangov achieved with Michael
Chekhov that he asked Vakhtangov to work with him
on his role of Salieri. It was a unique combination—
Stanislavski acting and Vakhtangov directing.

When the Habima Studio group, whose performers
spoke Hebrew, came to Moscow from the provincial
Polish town of Bialystok, they asked Stanislavski to
guide them. A few talks with Stanislavski made such
an impression on the leaders of the group that they

closed Habima and told the actors that they must study before they could reopen for public appearance. As a result, only a few remained; most of the members left, disappointed. Stanislavski recommended his best disciple, Vakhtangov, to teach the Habima actors the System. At the beginning of 1922, Vakhtangov staged their production of *The Dybbuk*, originally written in Russian by S. Anski. Stanislavski had suggested it to the Habima players, and the poet Bialik had adapted and translated the play into Hebrew.

In *The Dybbuk*, Vakhtangov guided the actors into a grotesque style without letting them forget Stanislavski's principles of inner truth. Grotesque, he said, was the style which expressed vividly the profound content of the play. His aim was to project the conflict of human feelings and destinies with inhuman laws that are the product of legends and superstitions, the world of fear affecting man's soul.

Vakhtangov interrupted the long nights of rehearsal only to swallow some bicarbonate, which was difficult to obtain in the hungry and cold Moscow of those days of revolution and civil war. The bicarbonate eased the pain of cancer for a while. With his coat on and a hot-water bottle at his side, Vakhtangov continued the work. When Habima lacked funds for sets and costumes, Vakhtangov would invite guests, entertain them, show some scenes, and ask for help; next day, Habima would have enough money. Sometimes I looked on as Vakhtangov, with unerring artistic intuition, showed the actors how people who spend their life in temples behave, how they eat, sleep, talk. He found a different theatrical rhythm for each character.

He demanded intonations that could be understood without an understanding of Hebrew. "Forget the superfluous imitation of life," he said. "Theater has its own realism, its own truth. This truth is in the truth of experiences and emotions that are expressed on stage with the help of imagination and theatrical means. Everything must be brought to the spectators with nothing but the colorful devices of theater." Every moment was given the utmost expressiveness, and all the symbols of the play were made clear. Vakhtangov gave birth to a theater of profound thought and experience united with powerful imagination in a variety of forms.

The Dybbuk opened on January 31, 1922. Drama critics were full of praise: "Every gesture, every intonation, every step, pose, and acting detail is brought to such technical perfection that one can hardly imagine anything superior. . . ." "Each moment was perfect, the most precise, the most absolute. . . ." "We saw theater in the precise, pure, and liberated meaning of the word. . . ."

While staging *The Dybbuk*, Vakhtangov, gravely ill, his pain increasing every day, directed at the First Studio, where he also performed in *The Deluge*, in addition to directing his own Third Studio. In the spring of 1920, Vakhtangov had become interested in Schiller's *Turandot*; later, he preferred Carlo Gozzi's original version. In *Turandot*, Vakhtangov wanted the audience to feel as if they were present at a feast. "No feast, no performance. Our work is senseless if there is no holiday mood, if there is nothing to carry the spectators away. Let us carry them away with our youth, laughter, and improvisation," said Vakhtangov. Actors worked on each word, gesture, and intonation until it seemed absolutely spontaneous, as if improvised.

During rehearsals of *Turandot*, actors competed in invention. A scarf became a beard; a lampshade became the emperor's hat; breadbaskets, spoons, and so on became parts of theatrical costumes. A typewriter and modern suitcases were used. Vakhtangov chose the best, and eventually *Turandot* took on the pure holiday mood he wanted. The matchless Vakhtangov brought to the stage a beautiful lightness. It was not a false theatricality, a director's whim; more than ever, Vakhtangov demanded the truth of inner experiences, and led his performers toward a vivid, colorful, internally full *theater*.

Rehearsals of *Turandot* started after eleven p.m., when his own performance ended, and lasted until about eight in the morning. Though I was not in its cast at the time, I never missed a rehearsal. Vakhtangov's dedication to the theater, his inexhaustible creative energy, overwhelmed me. His demands for discipline were so severe that actors were actually afraid of him. We knew that Vakhtangov had arrived by the sudden silence in the Studio. He could bring actors to elation with his praise, and I saw them weep over his cruel criticism. Vakhtangov's sparkling, ironical humor, his sharp intelligence, artistic sense, limitless energy, and, above all, his hatred of all that was vulgar, commanded admiration and respect. He was the trusted and respected leader.

Mortally ill, Vakhtangov demanded joy and infectious gaiety from the actors. "Actors must have joy in their hearts from the feeling of the stage. Without this, theater is a layman's pastime"—that was his belief. Occasionally he would grasp his side and swallow some bicarbonate; often, as soon as the pain eased a little, he went on stage to demonstrate to actors, moving with lightness. Vakhtangov hurried; he knew that he was not going to live long. I shall never forget his rehearsals: never satisfied, he sometimes canceled in a second what had been achieved during long nights; continually searching for truth and force, he made each rehearsal new.

In February 1922, Vakhtangov was ill with pneumonia. He was in the Third Studio with a temperature of 103 degrees, working on the lighting for *Turandot*. At four a.m., when the young actors were utterly exhausted, he ordered a run-through of the whole play. He seemed to know that this would be the last time he would see his masterpiece. After the run-through, when everyone else had gone home, Vakhtangov, too tired too move, lay down in his office for a few hours.

On February 27, 1922, a solemn dress rehearsal was held—the first performance of *Turandot*, ordered by Vakhtangov for Stanislavski. Vakhtangov's teachers and students were present: Stanislavski, Nemirovich-Danchenko, the actors of the Moscow Art Theater and of its Studios, including the Habima Studio group. Vakhtangov himself was at home, dying.

At the first intermission Stanislavski telephoned to Vakhtangov, and at the second break he hired a sleigh and went to his home. The performance was not to continue until Stanislavski's return.

"I wanted the actors to live truthfully, really cry and laugh. Do you believe in them?" Vakhtangov asked Stanislavski.

"Your success is brilliant," Stanislavski replied. He returned to the theater, and *Turandot* went on. At the end Stanislavski said to the actors, "In twenty-three years of the Moscow Art Theater's existence, there have been few triumphs such as this one. You have found what many theaters have sought in vain for a long time."

On the next evening, February 28, *Turandot* had its opening. "Having conquered stage naturalism, *Turandot*, with all its theatricality, is impregnated with true inner life, is filled with soul to the brim. . . ." wrote a drama critic.

"Fantastic" or "theatrical" realism was the name Vakhtangov gave to the art that he strove for. He believed that an actor who lives the inner experiences of a character must embody them with creative imagination. That is what Stanislavski teaches us, he said, and he quoted the master: "The truth on stage is not what happens in real life, but what could happen." Vakhtangov believed that the means for building the inner life had to be learned, and that the form and expression, dictated by contemporary life, had to be created with the help of imagination.

Vakhtangov could not endure formlessness. He always strove for the most precise, rich, inwardly full, and expressive external form for the particular dramatic work in question. He strove to eliminate triviality and to create new forms through the most imaginative means. His aim was the synthesis of imaginative sculptural form and inner truth. "Inner content dissipates if the controlling form is weak," he said. "Never stop searching, and cherish the form which discloses the inner content." Humor, a carefree smile, tragedy, deep thought—all nuances were united in an artistic whole in his acting and his staging. He impressed his audience with the depth of thought in his productions.

It should be noted that during the short years of Vakhtangov's creative life he was extremely interested in the work of Vsevolod Meyerhold (1874–1940), the famous experimenter whose daring productions provoked heated arguments.° This brilliant director left the Moscow Art Theater to fight a revolution of his own. Meyerhold's ambition was to invent sensational new stage laws. He never repeated himself. Contrary to Stanislavski, who wanted the spectators to lose themselves in the atmosphere of the play, Meyerhold wanted the audience never to forget that they were in a theater. Vakhtangov thought that Meyerhold, in his own way, strove for the same objective as Stanislavski: that of eliminating everything trivial. Meyerhold's extraordinary imagination and feeling for form impressed Vakhtangov, who wrote in his diary, "Each of his productions is a new theater. Every one of them could have a whole new theatrical direction." However, Vakhtangov thought that Meyerhold often acted purely from a desire to destroy the old, that he often imposed a form which had little to do with the essence

---

° Meyerhold's theory of "biomechanics" was based on the teachings of the American psychologist William James.

of the play, and that his greatest handicap was in his work with the actors, because he was not always able to attain the truth of genuine experience. Meyerhold, who was himself an actor, did not, however, know an actor's organic nature. He could give an actor a brilliant external pattern but could not help him to fill the role with inner life. Though Meyerhold eliminated triviality, Vakhtangov thought his theater dead, without emotion.

Vakhtangov was a great, daring artist who left his own distinctive mark on all his creations. Whereas Stanislavski searched more than forty years for answers to the problems of actors and directors and built a theater of true significance, Vakhtangov's creative life lasted only five enormously fruitful years. But his achievement was a product of his understanding of the vital value of Stanislavski's teachings.

There never was any break between the two great artists. Both strove for truth of content, truth of meaning, and both dreamed of a vivid theatrical form. Vakhtangov continued the search for form started by Stanislavski, who, amazed by his own discoveries, dedicated his life to developing and formulating his miraculous laws for the inner technique of acting. Those who speak of a break between Stanislavski and Vakhtangov are those who do not understand Stanislavski. Vakhtangov fought on Stanislavski's side with passion. Stanislavski discovered a scientific theory which pointed the way to endless experiment and further discoveries. Vakhtangov followed the signs faithfully and helped to move the Stanislavski System forward. The deductions which he made from the

System have given the theater greater techniques of acting. Although Vakhtangov's productions were experimental, his work was a milestone in the history of the Moscow Art Theater, and he had a profound influence on world theater.

Vakhtangov wrote to Stanislavski: "March 29, 1919. . . . I thank life for the opportunity of knowing you. . . . I do not know . . . anyone superior to you. In art I love the truth of which you speak and which you teach. . . . You said once, 'The Moscow Art Theater is my citizen's service to Russia.' . . . The symbol of every artist is in your words. I am your humble student. . . . I feel unworthy to show you my work. . . ."

On a photograph of himself which he gave to Vakhtangov, Stanislavski wrote: "To my dear friend, beloved disciple, talented colleague, the only heir, the first to answer the call, who believed in new ways in art, and who worked hard to introduce our principles into life, wise teacher who created schools and educated actors, the inspirer of many groups, the talented director and actor, creator of new principles of the revolutionary art, the future leader of the Russian theater." Stanislavski was known never to flatter. He meant what he said. Vakhtangov was not one of Stanislavski's disciples; he was *the* disciple.

Vakhtangov died at the age of thirty-nine, on May 29, 1922, at nine fifty-five p.m. The news of his death reached the Moscow theaters at once, and all audiences rose in tribute.

Index